Three Plays

Demons

Act

Terminal 3

**Other Chaucer Press Books by Lars Norén
Translated from Swedish to English by
Marita Lindholm Gochman**

Two Plays: And Give Us the Shadows and
Autumn and Winter (Spring 2013)

Plays: Blood and *War* (Fall 2014)

Three Plays

Demons

Act

Terminal 3

by

Lars Norén

Translated by

Marita Lindholm Gochman

Chaucer Press Books
An Imprint of Richard Altschuler & Associates, Inc.

Los Angeles

Distributed by University Press of New England

The translation cost for this book was supported by a grant from the Swedish Arts Council.

ISBN-13: 978-1-884092-88-6

Library of Congress Control Number: 2014934541
CIP data for this book are available from the Library of Congress

Chaucer Press Books is an imprint of Richard Altschuler & Associates, Inc.

Cover Design: Josh Garfield

Printed in the United States of America

Distributed by University Press of New England
1 Court Street
Lebanon, New Hampshire 03766

In Celebration of Lars Norén's 70th Birthday on
May 9, 2014

To Len

With deep love and gratitude for sharing your passion for the
theater and for your endless support in my quest to do justice to a
great playwright

Contents

Foreword

by

Stan Schwartz

Lars Norén and Musicality

One may approach the work of Lars Norén from any number of angles: psychological, sociological, political even—and they'd all be fitting. But I would like to take a more poetical approach—equally appropriate, given that Norén is a poet of the stage—and talk about musicality.

Norén has been writing plays for nearly half a century and I have been following his work for about fifteen years. It was at that time that I officially started looking quite closely at the contemporary Swedish theatre scene and writing about it. My explorations were mostly centered in Stockholm, but thanks to the privilege of being invited to participate in three consecutive iterations over six years of the Swedish Theatre Biennial, I had the opportunity to watch theatre from all over Sweden. Since it is absolutely accurate to say that Norén is the most important contemporary Swedish playwright since August Strindberg, it was inevitable that our paths would eventually cross.

I expected our intersection would be strictly figurative but, in fact, it turned out to be, happily, literal: We did a lengthy and fascinating interview in 2003 for the Swedish newspaper *Expressen.* Although the interview was ostensibly about his then-current play *Details,* other arguably more important issues were discussed besides the specifics of that play. In retrospect, this wasn't the slightest bit surprising. Any proper conversation with Norén turns into a poetic, free-associational give-and-take about many things, running the gamut from ordinary daily minutiae to the so-called Big Questions. I think it is one of the playwright's key aesthetic strategies, in the most general sense, to collapse the false mutual exclusivity of these two basic categories: he finds the cosmic in everyday small details at the same time he breaks down elusive philosophical abstractions into precise and discrete actions that an actor can play and an

xi

audience can immediately comprehend. In this regard, he is in some ways related to his Norwegian fellow playwright, Jon Fosse, and I suspect it is no accident that Norén translated Fosse's play *Someone is Going to Come* for a Riksteatern production in 2002, directed by Eirik Stubø. I might add it was a riveting evening of theatre.

But my own personal interaction with Norén went beyond a single interview. Surprisingly, he invited me on two separate occasions to attend his rehearsals at Riks (he directs plays as well as writes them). In the first instance, he was staging *The Seagull*, and in the second, he was directing his own play *Kyla*. The first play is Chekhov's classic from 19th century Russia, and the second is Norén's own dramatization, loosely based on a real-life incident, of the brutal murder of a young Korean immigrant by 3 neo-Nazi thugs in modern Sweden. The two plays could not be more different, and yet, I was struck by a particular quality common to both rehearsals: musicality. In both cases, the text was treated (more intuitively than consciously, I'm guessing) as a musical score whereby the rhythms of the dialogue were of paramount importance. The actors functioned, in a sense, as musicians whose instruments were their voices and movements. Norén would move around, watching carefully, or more importantly, listening carefully, as if he could best intuit the actors' intentions by simply listening to the rhythms of their speech. Most strikingly, he had a tendency to move his arms in a way that was absolutely evocative of a maestro conducting an orchestra.

Which brings me to the three plays in this collection, the second volume of Norén plays to be translated by Marita Gochman. Although an English translation of a single Norén play has popped up from time to time (though pretty rarely, one hastily adds), Marita has taken it upon herself to translate nearly 25 Norén plays, making her the foremost English translator of Noren's dramatic output. Consequently, it was as inevitable that our paths would cross as it was that Norén and I would intersect. We met for the first time in connection with her translation of *Details*—it comprised an essential component of my homework as I was preparing for my interview with Norén on the subject of the Royal Danish Theatre's visit to New York in 2003 with their production of the play. As directed by Bille August—who does have some superb films under his belt—the Royal Danish Theatre's production did not quite catch the musicality in the text as much as it might have. On the other hand, the later Dramaten production directed by Eva Bergman (in the original Swedish, naturally) was both poetic and haunting, and the interaction of the four actors genuinely felt like the interweaving of finely-tuned instruments in a string quartet.

Norén's musicality is also present in these three plays, even though they are rather different from each other. *Demons*, from 1982, is an early-ish domestic drama (some might say psychodrama) heavily influenced by Edward Albee, specifically, *Who's Afraid of Virginia Woolf*. It operates well within the realm of psychological realism, but the dialogue, one moment hilarious, the next moment harrowing, possesses an unmistakable musicality. This musicality was especially emphasized to haunting and luminous effect in Thomas Ostermeier's revival a few years ago for the Schaubühne in Berlin. (And as you would expect, Marita's translation was invaluable in my appreciation of that marvelous evening.) *Act* (2000) and *Terminal 3* (2006) are far sparser, minimalist even, and imbued with an almost dream-like hyper-realism that calls to mind Pinter (the Pinter influence in *Terminal 3* is particularly strong). And the Pinter connection, by definition, also means that the ghost of Samuel Beckett cannot be too far off in the wings, watching and smiling knowingly. Everyone knows just how much the waxing waning music of human speech is absolutely fundamental to the work of those two giants of late-20th century theatre, and it is not taking anything away from Norén's gifts to say he follows arguably as much in their footsteps as he does vis-à-vis Strindberg's visionary work.

Which makes it all the more puzzling to me why Norén is not better known and performed in English-speaking theatre. His work simply cannot nor should not be construed as somehow alien or different from what an English-speaking audience would expect from—or indeed, enjoy—in an evening at the theatre. Given the chance, an English-speaking audience would surely recognize the play, the characters, and most importantly, themselves in what they saw transpiring on stage before them. As it turns out—big surprise!—Norén follows Hamlet's advice to the Players quite well. He does indeed—to paraphrase the Danish Prince— hold up a formidable mirror to nature and show the very age and body of the time his form and pressure. And it behooves us to take a serious look at that reflection. And Marita's tireless translation efforts are obviously fundamental to that endeavor.

In closing, allow me to return for a moment to Norén's *Seagull* rehearsal. At a certain point, the actors stopped playing the scene in question, music was put on and everyone took to dancing for awhile, as a kind of freeing-up/relaxation exercise. I had the impression this "dance break" was a somewhat regular occurrence. (And let's face it, it's particularly fitting for Chekhov.) If memory serves correctly, any crew members or other non-actor-types who happened to be on hand were also encouraged to join in. I can't quite recall now if any did, but here's the one thing I do remember quite vividly: Norén invited me to join in on the dancing as well. My immediate response was to graciously decline. But the actors—an utterly charming and supremely talented bunch—cajoled me until I just couldn't say no, and so I awkwardly made my way on to the playing area and danced with everyone. I think it was an old-fashioned waltz. Whatever it was, for a short and wonderful while, I was no longer simply observing the Norén universe. I was actually in it and part of it. And it was a very special place to be.

Stan Schwartz
New York City
January 2014

Translator's Introduction

by

Marita Lindholm Gochman

In Lars Norén's recently published book about his life, *A Dramatist's Diary*, totaling more than twelve hundred pages, I came across a thought he shared with readers that I think expresses what the three plays in this book represent. He wrote, "I'm longing for a spiritual, non-religious theater—a more serious theater, a theater with a deeper analysis of our human condition."

It seems to me that Lars has always aimed for a more serious theater. For the last several decades, he has primarily written plays about the many ills in society, often set in his homeland, Sweden. He has looked closely at mental health issues and the care of the mentally disabled, problems of old age and end-of-life situations. He has spent time inside the Swedish prison system as a visiting playwright, investigating the conditions of the inmates from within. He has always been, and still is, politically engaged. He cares deeply about world events, and his thinking is firmly grounded in the intellectual Swedish "left." It has often been said that Norén's plays represent the conscience of Sweden. I have had the privilege and honor of working with Lars since 1982, primarily translating his plays from Swedish to English. I can attest to the fact that in his writing he always presents a deep analysis of the human condition.

His concern for the human condition is reflected in his continual reading of philosophy—including from the old Greeks, Heidegger, and Simone Weil—which, he says in his diary, is as important as breathing; and amazingly, he reads the works of most of the philosophers in their original language. It seems to give him great joy to try to "crack open," to understand, the original thought in its original language, which leads to the issue of translation.

Working on translations of plays, the translator is always trying to get to the original "thought," but that thought often must "transcend" the literal and manifest or express itself as a language the characters speak. Stated otherwise, while words are extremely important, of course, that doesn't mean the literal translation of a word necessarily is the "right" word for the situation or the character.

In working on the translations of the three plays in this book, I realized how much Lars's writing has changed from the time he wrote *Demons* to the more recent *Terminal 3. Terminal 3* is so sparsely written that at times I had to add words in order to make the lines understandable for an American audience, while in *Demons* I had to remove words and sentences.

The three plays selected for this book of Norén translations represent three very different periods in his playwriting. The play *Demons* was written in 1982. It's a young man's work, where the influences of Edward Albee and Harold Pinter are strongly felt. *Demons* has become one of those plays that virtually the whole world has discovered and embraced. There have been productions in Western Europe, Eastern Europe, Scandinavia, Australia, Japan, and South America, although not in North America at the time of this writing.

The play reflects circumstances that are universal to young, self-involved couples wherever they live on this planet; and the final part of the play can be interpreted as an expressionistic epiphany, which gives the director and the actors a wide variety of options with which to work. It is also a very humorous play, a play that can very easily transform itself into a farce. I think Lars would welcome any interpretation a director might bring to it.

The one-act play *Act*, written in 2000, is a two-character play set in a German prison. A female inmate, supposedly a terrorist, has been brought into a medical office within the prison in order to undergo a physical examination due to the fact that she is on a hunger strike. The interaction between prisoner and prison doctor becomes a contemplation of German "guilt," years after the Second World War. The play also finds a way to shed a light on the Nazi atrocities that had occurred. The power struggle between doctor and patient is ferocious and engaging. *Act* is a powerful and pertinent play, highlighting the complications of dealing with terrorists, whether they are ultra-Islamists or anti-capitalist fanatics. I think Lars is saying that, in all probability, there always will be a "Guantanamo Bay situation" somewhere on this earth.

Terminal 3 (2006) belongs to a series of plays that Lars has been working on for a number of years. The locations for the plays are mostly set in hospitals, care facilities, or psyche wards. The characters are often afflicted by physical or mental illnesses. Lars is shining a bright light on how far we still have to go, even in an enlightened country such as Sweden, before we can find real empathy and humanity in our welfare systems.

Terminal 3 is a lovely, quiet play. We meet a young couple in a hospital waiting room. They are there for the birth of their first child. A middle-aged couple arrives. They have been asked to come to the hospital to identify the body of their dead son. Eventually we come to understand that the couples are the same couple, only at different stages of their lives.

The sometimes extraordinary loneliness that our time seems to bring, the carelessness and ignorance of youth, the alienation that paralyzes and leads to anxiety and depression in many of us—all of that is captured, and not without a lovely sense of humor, in this spiritual play.

Based on my several decades of working with Lars and translating over twenty-five of his plays from Swedish to English, I can well confirm what he writes in *A Dramatist's Diary* about his work, personal life, political concerns, and quotidian activities, such as busily working in the Japanese garden of his country home on the island of Gotland in the Baltic Sea, conscientiously selecting just the right colors of gravel.

As regards his work, the words do not always flow easily for him when he is writing, and sometimes he experiences anxiety at not being able to write, of not having enough time to write, of his desperate need to write. Traces of scenes and characters are constantly dancing around in his head. It seems that several plays are always taking shape within him, many beginning as visual images during afternoon naps.

In his personal life, Lars has fallen in and out of love, had several children, including one recently, and fretted about being much too old for fatherhood. Nonetheless, he has fallen head-over-heels in love with his baby daughter, feels he never finds enough time for her, and worries that he will die before she gets to know him.

Although he is often lonely, he can't seem to be able to live with anyone. He often worries about money, but his desire for things such as expensive clothing and custom-made furniture can't be quelled. He's also very generous toward his own family, which is an expensive habit as well.

Transience and death are never far from his mind, because, as he writes in his diary, "We will soon be dead. We only live for a day." As regards his own death, he's aware that having been a heavy smoker since the age of fourteen he's a prime victim, but he has recently given up the habit, and one only hopes he can continue to do so.

Lars is also extremely concerned about politics, of course, both at home and on a global scale. In particular, he is deeply conflicted over the fate of Israel; he questions the actions of the United States around the world; and he is disturbed that in Sweden there is a "dumbing-down" of the middle class and obsession by the media with both celebrities and their empty lives and sordid crime stories reported in gory detail by the evening papers.

Despite his personal and political preoccupations and concerns, Lars is an artist who is always working, always creating—someone who never stops thinking about the next play, the next book, or the next collection of poetry. Although he is a complicated artist in the "last act" of his life, he still feels like the child—the child he always stands up for in his plays, the child who was misunderstood and mistreated by his parents, who couldn't deal with someone with his mind and imagination. He often thinks about his parents, now with compassion and love, and, perhaps, one could say forgiveness, but never without the "child" making himself heard.

Demons

Characters

Katarina, 36 years old, married to Frank

Frank, 38 years old

Jenna, 36 years old, married to Tomas

Tomas, 37 years old

The setting is an apartment in Stockholm in 1982.

SCENE ONE

The stage is dark. We hear Italian music. Anna Oxa is singing "Un'altra Me." The light comes up on Katarina. She is on her knees, her hand outstretched, as if she was about to feed an invisible bird. She seems to be in her own world. She is crying. She is smoking and dropping her ashes but doesn't care. A transistor radio on top of a plastic table is playing. She is dressed in a white bathrobe, the same color as a dove we see on the floor in front of her. She calls out for the bird to come to her. Carefully she walks to the open window and releases it. Katarina turns off the radio, sits down in silence, then walks over to the bathroom. The front door opens. Frank kicks over the telephone, which has been left on the floor in the hallway. He is carrying several packages and a plastic bag. He puts them down and turns on the light in the hallway.

KATARINA
(*from the bathroom*) Is that you? . . . Frank? . . . Frank! (*pause*) What's going on? (*a little concerned*) Is that you?

FRANK
No. (*He looks at the plastic bag and picks it up, unsure of what to do with it.*)

KATARINA
Why the hell aren't you answering me!

FRANK
(*calmly*) I guess I don't feel like it.

KATARINA
What did you say?

FRANK
I don't know. (*puts the plastic bag on the plastic cocktail cart, wipes away some cigarette ashes from the radio, which sits on top of the cart*) Katarina, how the hell do you manage to get ashes on the radio?

(*pause*)

KATARINA

I'm in here.

FRANK

You are?

KATARINA

You're late!

FRANK

(*is hanging up his coat*) Yes, I know.

KATARINA

(*opens the bathroom door*) You're late, I said.

FRANK

(*stands in the doorway and looks at her for a while, then with sudden tenderness*) Hello, darling. Am I late?

KATARINA

What do you think?!

FRANK

I have no idea what time it is.

KATARINA

So!

(*pause*)

FRANK

I don't know.

KATARINA

What have you been up to?

FRANK

I've been with my mom.

KATARINA

Before you came home. What were you doing?

FRANK

Nothing.

(*pause*)

KATARINA

Don't just stand there. They could be here any minute. I've got to take a shower.

FRANK

Why don't you do that. (*He notices a postcard sticking up from the pocket of the bathrobe that Katarina has thrown on the floor.*) Did you get a postcard from David? (*pause*) From some island somewhere? Greece? (*hangs up the bathrobe*) What does he say? (*Katarina starts the shower.*) And what did you do today?

KATARINA

What?

FRANK

What did you do today?

KATARINA

What did I do today?

FRANK

Yes. (*louder*) I thought I had asked you to clean up a little.

KATARINA

What are you talking about?

FRANK

Weren't you going to clean up the place?

KATARINA

I have been cleaning. For hours.

FRANK

(*has gone to the hallway*) Do you mind if I mess it up a little. (*Frank goes back to the bathroom and caresses Katarina through the shower-curtain.*) You're beautiful. . . . I said that you're beautiful.

KATARINA

What did you say? (*pause*) You think so? Why do you think I'm beautiful?

(*Frank goes back to the rolling cart and rolls it into the living room. On the way he picks up stuff that she has dropped—cigarette filters, pieces of clothing. He turns on the radio and fetches a hammer and nails to hang a picture that has been leaning against the wall, but doesn't have time to put it up before he hears the sounds of glass crashing onto the floor in the bathroom. He waits while several smaller crashes are heard, then throws the hammer and nails in the easy chair, walks quickly over to the bathroom, and rips the door open.*)

FRANK

Well excuse me, but what the hell are you doing?

KATARINA

(*On her toes, she doesn't dare to move. There are pieces of glass in the sink and on the floor.*) I couldn't find the towel.

FRANK

So that's why you had to break the mirror?

KATARINA

No, the glass shelf under the mirror. It wasn't installed properly.

FRANK

It's been like that for nine years. Lucky for you it wasn't the mirror.

KATARINA

Even luckier for you. You use it more than I do.

FRANK

What the hell do you mean by that?

KATARINA

Nothing, Frank. It was an accident. (*is drying herself*) Did you make the call?

FRANK

Look. It looks terrible. (*pause*) This is terrible.

KATARINA

Did you make the call?

FRANK

That's what I think. (*brings the vacuum cleaner from the hallway*) Do you hear what I'm saying? Don't you hear what I'm saying?

KATARINA

Oh yes, I heard you nine years ago. So, you didn't make the call?

FRANK

(*laughs*) Oh, that. Don't even think he'd be able to help you.

KATARINA

Not me. You are the one who needs help.

FRANK

Yeah, and that would help you, you think?

KATARINA

Yes.

FRANK

It won't. If I got help I'd be leaving you right away.

KATARINA

I know.

FRANK

Darling, hell, I'm the one who'll be leaving you, not you me. You'll have to deal with me until I'm strong enough to leave you. That's how it is. (*pause*) How the hell do you do it? (*pause*) Look at this. How?

KATARINA

For God's sake, don't be such a nag. I promise I'll get it fixed tomorrow, as long as you shut up about it! Please get me a pair of shoes so that I can get out of here.

FRANK

Then why don't you take care of the glass shelf in the refrigerator at the same time. Let's see, it's only been three years since you broke it.

KATARINA

Who the hell can stand living like this?

FRANK

You. You can stand living like this.

KATARINA

What fucking glass shelf?

FRANK

(*with emphasis on every word*) The one that's in the lower part of the refrigerator, where we keep our vegetables. You know exactly which one I mean.

KATARINA

(*wearing a bathrobe*) Oh, that one.

FRANK

Is it broken or what?

KATARINA

I forgot about that one. I thought you did too. My shoes.

FRANK

Forgotten maybe, but not forgiven. . . . So where am I supposed to put my shaving stuff now?

KATARINA

(*puts back half the shelf that had fallen into the sink*) There, your part didn't break. As always. (*puts back his bottles of Kouros and Nino Cerutti, his toothbrushes, and so on*) Please get me my shoes.

FRANK

What did you say?

KATARINA

Go and get my shoes.

FRANK

Why don't you get them yourself?

KATARINA

I'll cut myself.

FRANK

So?

KATARINA

You're sick.

FRANK

Don't you look at me like that with your small, crinkly, pig eyes, sorry.
So . . . where are they, where did you put them?

KATARINA

I'll get them myself.

FRANK

No, stay there. You'll cut yourself. I'll get them. (*He leaves and comes
back with a pair of black high-heeled shoes.*) Did you mean these?

KATARINA

No, I didn't, thank you.

FRANK

(*thinking of the high heels*) Last night I had a dream about a big clock,
and that my cock, just the head of the penis itself, was sticking straight
out where the number one is; and the hand indicating the minutes was a
long razorblade showing five minutes to twelve.

KATARINA

(*climbing out of the tub into her shoes*) Ugh, now I feel clean again. (*She
picks up a pair of panties and starts to put them on, turned away from
him. He stands there looking at her.*) At least I'll have loads of panties.

FRANK

What big hands you have.

KATARINA

I do?

(*pause*)

FRANK

I remember in the beginning, when we'd been holding hands some evening, that it was like taking out the dog. (*pause*) Really, when?

KATARINA

What?

FRANK

(*dealing with the vacuum cleaner*) When will you have loads of panties?

KATARINA

(*is putting on hand cream*) If we divorce. Is that the phone? (*Katarina goes out to the hallway.*)

FRANK

How the hell would I know? Don't talk like that.

KATARINA

Like what?

FRANK

What do you mean?

KATARINA

God, what did I say now? Frank. (*into the phone*) Hello.

FRANK

This is what you said; you said that you'll have loads of panties when we divorce.

KATARINA

Did I say that? I don't remember. (*hangs up the phone*)

FRANK

That's a sentence I won't easily forget.

KATARINA

(*goes to the closet*) Either I'll kill you, or you'll kill me, or we'll leave each other, or we'll continue to live like this. You choose.

FRANK

I can't choose. You choose.

KATARINA

Did I really say "when we divorce"?

FRANK

That's what I heard.

KATARINA

Well, that's what I'd do if you didn't make that call. Divorce you. Everything must end sometime.

FRANK

(*He is in the living room looking for an outlet for the vacuum cleaner cord.*) Really.

KATARINA

Did you call?

FRANK

Guess.

KATARINA

My guess is that you called.

FRANK

Yes.

KATARINA

Lucky for you. (*She takes the hairdryer from the closet shelf, gives him a kind smile, is about to pass him, and caresses him lightly.*)

FRANK

(*touches her private parts*) Sorry.

KATARINA

(*after a pause*) Why did you do that?

FRANK

I don't really know. I'm never aware of her until she's hidden.

KATARINA

(*almost motherly, pretend motherly*) Are you hungry, tired, are you sad? . . . What?

FRANK

No. . . . So, I'm not allowed to touch you there?

KATARINA

(*pause*) Be my guest.

FRANK

(*forces her to sit on the table*) Does this feel good?

KATARINA

Sort of.

FRANK

Yes?

KATARINA

(*pause*) No. (*without any expression*) Are you done?

FRANK

Yes, I was done a long time ago. I'm completely done. (*Katarina passes him, walks into the bedroom. He remains where he is, looking at her. The phone rings.*) Who's going to clean up the mess now? (*picks up the phone*) Hello. (*turns off the radio*) Let me look. (*goes to the kitchen, opens the door of the kitchen cabinet*) Sure you can. Come up anytime. (*He puts the phone on top of the refrigerator, drinks a glass of milk, takes out a package of rice, and puts it in the hallway.*)

KATARINA

(*In the bedroom holding her hairdryer, she puts the cord in the outlet, starts the dryer, and sits down on the bed. Frank comes in carrying a paper bag and turns on the light.*) Please turn off the light.

FRANK

What did you say?

KATARINA

Turn off the light.

FRANK

How?

KATARINA

Turn the switch . . . like this.

FRANK

Don't you feel well?

KATARINA

Well, I'm just cold. I'm shaking.

FRANK

I don't see it.

KATARINA

You never see anything.

FRANK

There's nothing wrong with my eyes. My eyes are too good. I see too well.

KATARINA

May I have a cigarette?

FRANK

(*gives her a cigarette, lights it for her*) Is there anything else you would like? No? . . . You know, since it's so nice and warm maybe we can serve the coffee on the balcony. (*sits down at the end of the bed*)

KATARINA

You didn't light it. I might as well light it myself. (*She takes his lighter, lights her cigarette, then drops the lighter on the floor.*)

FRANK

(*picks up her coffee cup off the floor*) This is your coffee cup. May I try to put it over there, on the table?

KATARINA

Yes, try.

FRANK

Good. . . . I hate when you're like this.

KATARINA

Really, how am I?

FRANK

Your arrogant way of just dropping the lighter like that.

KATARINA

I know. (*spreads her legs*) What's so arrogant about that?

FRANK

(*mean spirited*) Are you expecting someone?

KATARINA

Yes, your brother and his wife. (*She turns on the hair dryer. Frank smiles, but we know it isn't a smile.*) Are you sick?

FRANK

(*Sitting on the bed again, he takes a shoebox out of the paper bag and starts to open it.*) No, I'm happy. (*pause*) Why do you ask?

KATARINA

Why? (*turns off the dryer*) Because your mother is dead?

FRANK

(*without raising his voice*) Cut it out. Stop it.

KATARINA

I know I'll be very nice when my mother decides to take a hike, and that'll probably happen before we know it, as many incurable diseases as she imagines she has. (*turns on the hairdryer*) Because this couldn't possibly have anything to do with us, right? (pause) Am I right? (*pause*) I said am I right?

FRANK

Why are you yelling? I'm right here.

KATARINA

But you don't hear me.

FRANK

Do you?

KATARINA

(*turns off the hairdryer*) Does it have anything to do with us?

FRANK

(*indifferent*) That you're yelling?

KATARINA

That you're so happy. It couldn't possibly be? (*turns on the hairdryer*)

FRANK

Why not? . . . I didn't say that I was happy.

KATARINA

Yes you did. You really did.

FRANK

I did? . . . Why did I do that?

KATARINA

Well, I don't know. (*throws the hairdryer on the bed without turning it off*) How do I look?

FRANK

(*looks at her*) Manic.

KATARINA

Thank you. (*Frank has been taking off his suede shoes and is putting on one of the new shoes.*) New shoes?

FRANK

(*quietly*) Old and manic.

KATARINA

Not brown, I hope?

FRANK

(*turns off the hairdryer*) Older and cleaner.

KATARINA

(*stands up*) Let me see. Hold them up. Frank, let me take a look?

(*pause*)

FRANK

No, I'm keeping them here in the box. With the lid on. (*stands up with one foot in the shoebox*)

KATARINA

Don't be embarrassed. You should have the shoes you like. Where are you going? (*Frank goes to the kitchen. He hides the shoebox in the refrigerator and walks over to the espresso machine. Katarina comes into the kitchen.*) Are you wearing brown shoes to the funeral?

FRANK

(*whistles*) It's not a funeral. It's a burial. Now Urnie is going into the dirt.

KATARINA

Which Urnie?

FRANK

The urn, the urn I mean.

KATARINA

Say urn, then. (*pause, looking for the shoebox in the kitchen cabinet*) Which Urnie?

FRANK

I don't know any Urnie.

KATARINA

So why do you want him dead then? (*pause*) Why are you so aggressive?

FRANK

Towards Urnie?

KATARINA

And me.

FRANK

I'm not that aggressive towards you.

KATARINA

No, not as much as you'd like to be!

FRANK

Oh no. (*He pauses, opens the refrigerator, and pours milk in his espresso cup.*) It suddenly hit me, if you were to have an affair, it would probably be with my best friend. Am I right? (*pause*) Wouldn't it? (*pause*) I guess that would be when you'd open up your little box? (*slams the refrigerator door shut*) Would you like a couple of expensive drops? (*means the espresso*) Why don't you answer me?

KATARINA

No thanks. (*Once again Frank starts to whistle. Katarina picks up a comb to comb her hair.*)

FRANK

What are you doing now?

KATARINA

Combing my hair.

FRANK

With a knife? (*Katarina discovers that she is holding a knife.*)

KATARINA

What is my problem?

(*pause*)

FRANK

On your gravestone there shouldn't be a dove, there should be a little rat.

KATARINA

Please, dear Frank . . .

FRANK

Sorry. I don't know what's wrong with me. What a terrible thing to say.

KATARINA

You think so?

FRANK

Yes.

(*pause*)

KATARINA

(*as if she was thinking of something else*) I love you. You know that.

FRANK

What did you say?

(*pause*)

KATARINA

I love you.

(*pause*)

FRANK

Yes, but what are you really saying?

KATARINA

Only that I love you. . . . (*Frank is looking down on the park below through the kitchen window. Katarina takes a cigarette out of Frank's breast pocket. He embraces her. They stand for a long time in silence. There's a knock on the door.*)

FRANK

I'll get it.

JENNA

(*in the doorway*) This is great. . . . Lucky for me, I always forget something. (*Frank takes the packet of rice from the shelf and closes the kitchen door.*) Every time I go shopping I always forget one thing. Every time it's the same. Just one thing, and I never discover it until I'm home, and then I think, what did I forget this time? That's the way it is every time, so I didn't discover it until just now. Isn't it strange that it's just one thing every time? Never two. And that I don't think about it until I get home? This time I forgot the rice.

FRANK

Yes, the rice, here it is. My pleasure.

JENNA

(*takes the packet of rice*) The rice that doesn't stick, but I'm really sticky.

FRANK

Yes, it's very warm.

JENNA

Yes, it's wonderful. I'll bring it back tomorrow. Should I just leave it by the door?

FRANK

No, no, keep it.

JENNA

I don't need that much.

FRANK

That's fine.

JENNA

Are you sure? We hardly ever eat rice. Thank you. I'd better run downstairs. Is Katarina around? Your apartment up here feels much cooler, I think. Do your radiators still make a lot of noise?

FRANK

Not during the summer, they're turned off.

JENNA

We can't even sleep downstairs. You go crazy. (*She leaves.*)

KATARINA

(*standing in the kitchen doorway*) What's going on?

FRANK

It's Jenna.

KATARINA

Really.

FRANK

(*looks at himself in the mirror*) She just wanted to borrow some rice.

KATARINA

Are you sure?

FRANK

You can never be really sure.

KATARINA

She would never even touch you.

FRANK

(*keeps turning the light on and off in the hallway*) No?

KATARINA

No, absolutely not. . . . She asked me why you always have to hug her. Do you know what she said? . . . Frank? . . . He's always looking at himself in the mirror. She's right of course. Are you nervous?

FRANK

No, not at all. No, I feel good, very good.

KATARINA

Yes, I feel good too, but as always, when I feel good, I feel a little bit bad too. (*She says it without making a joke, and goes to her closet. Frank is still only wearing socks.*) Are you wearing brown shoes tomorrow?

FRANK

Yes, I am.

KATARINA

I guess she won't notice.

FRANK

(*looks into the plastic bag sitting on the cocktail cart*) Well, better keep her here, so that I can keep an eye on her.

KATARINA

(*takes out a dress from the closet*) Do you think they would want something to eat?

FRANK

(*somehow in the same tone of voice*) No, if I know my brother he'll have eaten all the way up here and will only want a chair to fart in.

KATARINA

(*indifferent*) Couldn't you try not to terrorize him?

FRANK

Impossible. . . . His head is like a soccer ball—one has to keep kicking it. (*picks up the plastic bag again and looks into it*) Maybe I better put her in the hallway so that I don't forget her. (*Katarina passes him on her way to the bedroom and caresses him lightly on his cheek. Frank reacts as if he'd been hit.*) Sorry.

KATARINA

(*She stares at him. His reaction had been so strong, he didn't know why.*) I tried to touch you. (*pause*) I tried to caress you.

FRANK

I said I'm sorry. I didn't get it. I said I'm sorry. I didn't see what you were doing.

KATARINA

Well, then, forget it. (*goes into the bedroom*) Thank God there's a funeral so there'll be some people around. . . . I guess you won't be going to bed with a thriller and a glass of milk tonight. Tonight I'm going to have a good time; I'm not going to consider you at all. (*Frank is following her, holding the plastic bag. She's about to put on some makeup. Frank stands in the doorway.*) Wow, look at me. I look a lot older . . . older but cleaner.

FRANK

What was that, that thing you're not going to do?

KATARINA

Me? Nothing. Put on lipstick. (*sarcastically remembers*) Paint my small, crinkly, pig eyes. Incredibly mean.

FRANK

What did you mean by that? (*sits on the bed*) That you are not going to consider me at all? What do you mean by that?

KATARINA

Absolutely nothing. What time is it? Shouldn't they be here by now?

FRANK

That's enough, Katarina. (*louder*) It's enough. Tell me what you meant by that.

KATARINA

Nothing . . . I meant nothing.

FRANK

The hell you didn't, and I want to know. Tell me. (*even louder*) Tell me,
I said. Otherwise I'm leaving.

KATARINA

Yes, why don't you. (*smiles quickly*) And take your mommy with you.

FRANK

I can't believe it.

KATARINA

(*after a pause*) Frank . . .

FRANK

What the fuck! What did you really mean? (*stands up quickly*)

KATARINA

Dear Frank.

FRANK

Don't even try.

KATARINA

Why don't you calm down? (*after a pause*) Frank, no hitting, I beg you.

FRANK

What are you really saying?

KATARINA

You look exactly the way you do when you're wondering if it's a good
idea to hit me.

FRANK

You're crazy . . . completely crazy. I look like this, then? How?

KATARINA

Psychotic. Like a waiter with a flyswatter.

FRANK

I look like that? Right now?

KATARINA

Yes, you do, but you aren't going any further, are you? Not now when other people are coming and everything?

FRANK

No, absolutely not.

KATARINA

You're sure, are you?

FRANK

I'm not going to hit you. Not now. I'll hit you when you don't expect it. Now you expect it. That I'm going to hit you. But I'll wait. (*He is smiling as he puts on his shoes*) I'll wait to hit you until you don't expect me to hit you. (*determined pause*) Then I'll hit you.

KATARINA

Darling, let's quit fighting. (*looks up at him*) Can't we quit?

FRANK

Can can can we? But will will will we? (*The phone rings.*) The phone. (*He goes to the kitchen. We hear him talk. Katarina, alone in the bedroom, starts to cry, and is still crying when he comes back.*) Well, they aren't coming.

KATARINA

What?

FRANK

I said, they aren't coming.

KATARINA

Who? Who aren't coming?

FRANK

Well, whatever their names are. . . .

KATARINA

Your brother? He isn't coming? (*Frank is shaking his head in silence.*) What?

FRANK

No, I said.

KATARINA

Why not?

FRANK

Because they're spending the night at Three Shells in Sodertalje. A mo-
tel.

KATARINA

Why?

FRANK

He wants to watch a soccer match.

KATARINA

Why?

FRANK

I guess he's interested in it.

KATARINA

That can't be true.

FRANK

That's possible, but that's what he said. He said they'll be here tomorrow. (*Frank sits down on the bed.*)

KATARINA

What?

FRANK

He said that they'll be here tomorrow. What's so strange about that?
(*looks down into the plastic bag*) Yeah . . . why don't we have a little
orgy instead, you and me?

KATARINA

(*stands up*) Then I'm going out.

FRANK

Where?

KATARINA

Wherever. It doesn't batter at all.

FRANK

Batter? . . . You said batter, batter, batter. Why did you say batter?

KATARINA

(*stops in the bedroom door*) I can't take it anymore.

FRANK

You can't take it?

KATARINA

No.

FRANK

(*irritated*) No. (*pause*) What?

KATARINA

I've got to get out. Out of here.

FRANK

Why?

KATARINA

Not one more evening.

FRANK

No?

KATARINA

Not one more evening.

FRANK

Excuse me? (*silence*) Really . . . aha . . . may I ask where you're going?

KATARINA

Wherever. Whatever.

FRANK

Couldn't I come too, go out with you?

KATARINA

I want to go out by myself.

FRANK

So what am I supposed to do then?

KATARINA

I just don't have the strength to sit here one more evening and fight with you. It's true. (*She goes up to Frank and takes a cigarette and a lighter out of his breast pocket.*)

FRANK

Why don't we ask Jenna and Tomas to come up for a visit instead? I'm sure they aren't doing anything. On a Wednesday night and everything. It's a thought anyway. You like Tomas, don't you?

KATARINA

I do? No more than you like Jenna.

FRANK

No, that's what I meant. Sure I like her, I think she's nice. Don't you think she's nice?

KATARINA

She asked me why you always have to hug her.

FRANK

Yes, you told me. And what did you say then?

KATARINA

To piss me off.

FRANK

And what did she say then?

KATARINA

She laughed.

FRANK

So, what do you think? Why don't we ask them? I'll call and ask if they feel like coming up and have a drink with us. (*pause*) What do you say? I'll call them. Wouldn't that be nice? What do you think? So answer me.

(*Katarina shrugs.*) Well, then. (*He goes to the kitchen, brings the plastic bag, puts it on the cocktail cart, and makes the call. Katarina has put on a black dress. Frank comes back. He meets Katarina in the living room.*)

KATARINA

I guess they didn't want to?

FRANK

It sounded as if they'd been sitting around waiting for weeks for some-one to call.

KATARINA

Who did you talk to? Tomas? (*Frank takes the cologne out of the paper bag in the closet and splashes some on his face.*) Why did you say that I don't have to worry?

FRANK

I never said that. . . .

(*They are looking at each other.*)

KATARINA

Look at me.

FRANK

That's what I'm doing.

KATARINA

But you don't see me. (*encouraging*) Do you love me?

FRANK

(*indifferent*) You?

KATARINA

(*indifferent*) Yes. Do you love me?

FRANK

Yes. I love you. (*silence*) Very much. (*happily*) But I don't like you. . . . (*puts the cologne on the cocktail cart*) Not at all. I dislike you a lot. But I can't live without you.

KATARINA

Why not?

FRANK

I think I'll put mom up here on the shelf so you don't put your ashes on her. (*He puts the plastic bag on the shelf in the closet.*)

KATARINA

Put her in front of the mirror, then you'll have two mothers. When are you going to the psychiatrist?

FRANK

Who?

KATARINA

You said you'd called. I guess it's a she?

FRANK

In four years.

KATARINA

What?

FRANK

Four years.

KATARINA

What?

FRANK

Yeah, ha ha ha—there's a four-year wait. But I'm not going for the thing we've been talking about. I'm going because of my sinusitis. (*Frank goes over to the rolling table.*)

KATARINA

Four years.

FRANK

It'll go fast. *Rapido.* (*He turns on the cassette recorder and hears an Italian singer.*)

KATARINA

Good God. I can't. It won't work. It can't be true. Is it? What am I to do?

FRANK

Bo.

KATARINA

What?

FRANK

Bo!

KATARINA

What's that?

FRANK

Bo!

KATARINA

What the hell do you mean by that?! Who's that? Why the hell are you saying "bo"?

FRANK

It means "*tja*" in Italian.

KATARINA

Bo?

FRANK

Yes. Bo . . . bo.

KATARINA

(*picks up the cassette player*) Bo! Is this that fucking Italian whore that you . . . ? Gianna . . . Anna . . . she sucks . . .

FRANK

Still, you never forget her.

KATARINA

No, do you? (*throws the cassette player at Frank*)

FRANK

Okay, let's calm down.

KATARINA

What should I do?

FRANK

Whatever you want.

KATARINA

(*flatly*) Whatever I want?

FRANK

Whatever you yourself want. Is that so hard?

KATARINA

Yes, yes, it is.

FRANK

It is?

KATARINA

Yes, yes.

FRANK

Why?

KATARINA

(*calmly*) Because I, myself, am you.

FRANK

(*confused*) Dear Katarina . . . they'll be here in a little while. Please be a little happy.

KATARINA

(*the beginning of a breakdown*) You make me so unhappy. Afraid . . . and so confused. And empty. I just feel like running away . . . back to . . . back to . . .

FRANK

To where?

KATARINA

To you.

FRANK

Please don't cry when they get here. Then they'll think it's all my fault. So, stop it. Now . . . well, I suggest that you start living the kind of life you can't live with me (*sarcastically*) and start to accumulate everything you say I stop you from getting—but don't tie me down to this suggestion.

KATARINA

(*as if his words brought her back to the music of their relationship*) No, I can't. (*in a direct way*) Come over here. (*in a happy way*) So, come here then. Come over here, I said. Come to little, little me.

FRANK

(*makes a grimace*) Yeah, yeah, yeah, yeah, you really aren't so little.

KATARINA

Sure I am. But I'm still taller than you.

FRANK

No, you aren't.

KATARINA

Sure I am. Can't you see?

FRANK

That's not fair. You can't stand on top of my suede shoes. Don't you see that I'm taller than you?

KATARINA

You're right. But I'm not wrong either. (*Katarina kisses him. He responds; the kiss becomes sexual. She knows it. She caresses his neck, knowing that he'll react to that. She is reacting to his reaction. He puts his hand under her dress. It's all very erotic. They glide down on the floor. Frank pulls her underwear off.*) I don't want you to take this as a threat, but if you want me to I'll be your woman for the rest of our lives. (*There's a knock on the door.*) As long as I treat you like shit you'll stay with me. I know that.

FRANK

(*lets go of her*) There was a knock on the door.

KATARINA

Am I right? (*holds him tight*) Isn't that right?

FRANK

What?

KATARINA

(*in a direct and businesslike way*) As long as I treat you like shit you'll be tied to me. (*another knock on the door*) Am I right? (*takes a cigarette and the lighter out of Frank's breast pocket*) It sounds cruel, but right now I'm in the mood to be cruel. Please get the door.

SCENE TWO

(*a last knock at the door*)

FRANK

(*goes over and opens the door*) How was the rice?

JENNA

Hello Katarina, is this a real party? . . .

KATARINA

No, I'm just wearing this dress.

JENNA

Really great looking.

KATARINA

No really, do you really think so?

FRANK

How was the rice?

JENNA

Great looking. It's perfect on you.

KATARINA

Come in.

JENNA

So nice that you called. We were just sitting there watching a soccer match.

FRANK

Is Tomas still sitting there? (*pause*) What's the score?

JENNA

(*steps over the vacuum cleaner*) May I use the phone?

FRANK

What's the score?

KATARINA

The phone? Sure.

JENNA

(*distracted, to Katarina*) I've got to call Tomas.

FRANK

(*turns off the radio*) Why?

JENNA

(*goes into the living room*) Is it here? (*looks around*) How nice it is up here, not a lot of furniture everywhere. That's really nice, isn't it? May I use the phone?

KATARINA

Just follow the cord. (*Katarina is trying to get her underwear back from Frank's hand.*)

JENNA

Hello, it's me, Jenna. I'm up here now. You can bring it in there now, but put it down carefully so that you don't wake him up. (*She is almost whispering. Katarina is by the kitchen door.*) Are you in there now? . . . Not in the bed, then he might strangle himself. . . . Put it on the table. . . . Be quiet now so that I can hear.

FRANK

(*whispers*) What the hell is she doing?

JENNA

(*listens, smiles*) Oooooh, honey bun . . . he's sleeping so soundly. (*still whispering*) Are you coming up? Hurry. Don't forget to turn the TV off. Bye, darling. (*still holding the phone*) He's sleeping so soundly.

FRANK

(*by the kitchen door*) What are you two doing?

JENNA

Tomas just put the phone in the nursery by Wolfgang's crib so that we'll know if he wakes up. Then I'll just run downstairs.

KATARINA

That's very clever.

JENNA

He just ate.

FRANK

Aha. (*looks at the phone as if he was expecting a burp*) Do we have to speak softly?

JENNA

(*the whole time to Katarina*) Then I don't have to sit here and worry the whole time. We really hadn't planned on having another child this late in life, but I couldn't handle an abortion.

KATARINA

May I listen? (*takes the phone*)

FRANK

What's happening?

KATARINA

Sssh! Fantastic. I don't hear anything.

JENNA

I wouldn't have had the strength to go through an abortion, not now that we've seen the result. Then it's better to walk around like a zombie not knowing if it's day or night. (*smiles at Katarina, on her way into the bedroom*) Yesterday I forgot the code to get into our apartment. It's crazy. But from now on I'll always remember it, because Tomas told me it's the same as the year president Kennedy was murdered.

KATARINA
Why don't you sit down.

JENNA
Thank you. . . . Where?

FRANK
Should I get an ashtray?

JENNA
(*looks around, walks in different directions, turns to Katarina*) Would you, Katarina?

KATARINA
Yes, please. What did you say?

JENNA
(*at the table, still holding the phone*) Have managed an abortion?

KATARINA
I can't even manage to get pregnant.

JENNA
Really, well, don't worry, there are those who've been trying for ten years and then suddenly there's a child; and then there are those who can't. Have you tried to . . .

KATARINA
(*quickly*) Yes, everything.

JENNA
And then kept your legs straight up in the air right afterwards?

FRANK
(*returns, holding an ashtray*) No, life isn't fair.

JENNA
No, why should it be?

KATARINA

Sit down.

FRANK

Yes, sit in that beautiful chair. That one really is like one single move-
ment. (*shows with a gesture*)

JENNA

Oh, yes, it's really beautiful. Where did you get it?

KATARINA

(*She takes the ashtray and puts her ashes on the floor. Frank goes to the
bedroom.*) I hate fascist furniture like that one. I guess Frank's sperms
are too tired, or maybe they don't like me.

JENNA

(*almost sitting*) No, I don't dare to sit in it. Then I'll fall asleep.

KATARINA

And now I don't even want to . . . have kids, I mean.

JENNA

I don't know, I can't seem to really make it look nice down there,
however much I push the furniture around. No use when you have two
kids destroying everything. . . . But I think there's something wrong with
these apartments; you can't decorate them, you can't make them feel like
a home.

KATARINA

(*continues to put her ashes on the floor*) It's because the ceilings are so
fucking high.

JENNA

But it's nice here. This is how empty and clean I'd like ours to be.

KATARINA

Why can't you? But not grey. White, not grey.

FRANK

(*from the bedroom door after changing into a new shirt*) It's not grey.
It's an off-white.

KATARINA

You think so?

FRANK

Absolutely. The trim is glossy white, number eighty-five. Can't get any whiter than that.

KATARINA

The trim, yes, but what about all the rest?

JENNA

But you can't when you have little kids; they bring their goddamn toys everywhere.

KATARINA

It's never been white. Stockholm-grey maybe. Shitty-white probably.

JENNA

What a funny expression, "shitty-white."

FRANK

Where's your bedroom these days?

JENNA

What?

KATARINA

Why do you ask?

FRANK

I mean, where do you sleep?

JENNA

I hardly ever sleep . . . in the room in the back. But it doesn't work at all because we've had to put our bed straight across in order to open the door to get in, so now we are looking straight into the hallway at the mittens and boots and stuff. (*pause*) Because we can't close the door either. It's warped. It's so depressing. (*Jenna is looking into the bedroom.*) Our bedroom is green.

FRANK

Depressing.

JENNA

What? (*Jenna puts the phone on the cocktail cart. The receiver is off.*)

FRANK

Depressing.

JENNA

What?

FRANK

The word "depressing." Haven't heard it in a long time. By the way, are we disturbing you in any way?

JENNA

(*moving very slowly*) No, not at all, not that I've noticed.

KATARINA

What?

JENNA

No. We haven't heard anything. Are we disturbing you in any way?

FRANK

No, not at all. You're always so quiet.

JENNA

Well, yes, sounds travel mostly downwards. Our washing machine . . .

KATARINA

(*goes to the window*) No.

JENNA

I keep perspiring.

FRANK

Not at all.

JENNA

Since it's running twenty-four-seven.

FRANK

Uhm. (*charmingly*) We've also bought one.

JENNA

What kind?

FRANK

A tiny son of a bitch.

JENNA

I hope you'll tell us if we're disturbing you, I really do.

KATARINA

My guess is that we'd be the ones who've been disturbing you. (*A certain caution has crept into the conversation.*) Our screaming and hollering and slamming of doors and our blood stains on the stairs.

JENNA

But that was an accident.

FRANK

It was? Maybe next time it'll be through the window.

JENNA

Of course one fights now and then. We do too, I think.

KATARINA

Not Tomas, right? He seems so incredibly nice and kind.

JENNA

Kind? Yes, I'm not complaining. (*She gets quiet. They look at her but she continues as if she didn't want to continue.*) We hardly ever fight. . . . (*Katarina picks up a glass from the cocktail cart and goes to the kitchen. Jenna follows her and stops by the door. Frank puts away the vacuum cleaner.*) We both lack a sense of humor. When Tomas gets angry I just tell him I love him. If you just say the right words nothing happens. If you say "I love you" at the right moment, then there's no fighting.

FRANK

(*goes to the kitchen*) Are you thirsty? . . . I'm thirsty.

JENNA

It's so much brighter up here.

FRANK

Do you think so? (*takes a glass filled with wine from Katarina's hand*)

JENNA

(*after a while*) Yes.

FRANK

But I guess it's cozier down there.

JENNA

Much brighter. . . . very nice when it's raining that the windows can still be open. Do you also have pigeons pecking on the windows? I really like this city block. (*livelier*) We've everything around here—drugstore, post office, grocery store, tobacco store, liquor store—close to the subway and . . . (*looks out the kitchen window*) . . . down there is the park where the kids can play in the summer, learn to ride a bike. Where's Tomas?

KATARINA

Just be careful so they don't eat rat poison.

FRANK

The pigeons?

JENNA

The kids?

KATARINA

They've been putting rat poison even in the sandboxes. The rats have gotten so big lately. In Rome they put it out for the pigeons too—two different kinds of rat poison, one kind that makes the pigeons shrivel up, slowly but surely until they die from it, while the other kind makes them swell up like balloons. They swell up like balloons until they explode up in the air with big "poofs." It's true.

FRANK

Poofs?

KATARINA

Yes, poofs.

FRANK

(*surprised*) Not poofs. You must mean puffs?

KATARINA
(*while something bad is sneaking into her voice*) No—big, disgusting, bloated, fucking poofs.

JENNA
That's disgusting. Was it long ago . . . that you were in Rome? It's a beautiful city.

FRANK
Tell us about the rat guy, Katarina.

KATARINA
No.

FRANK
Please, tell us. It was so nice last night when we were in bed and you told me about the rat guy.

KATARINA
No, I said.

FRANK
Dear Katarina, tell us about the guy who stood buried in a hole in the ground where he couldn't move either his arms or his legs, with a little rat by his feet, a little hungry rat, who couldn't get out, so the little rat had to eat his way out through the guy's intestines and then crawl out of his mouth. Tell us that story. You tell it so well.

KATARINA
You tell it.

FRANK
I don't remember it.

KATARINA
Since it's about you. (*She goes to the kitchen.*)

FRANK
So, you both lack a sense of humor. Going from one thing to another, as they say. (*silence*)

JENNA

Well, very nice that you called. What do you think we should do?

FRANK

What? What we should do? Spend time together.

JENNA

(*absentmindedly*) It's been so long since I talked to a grown-up that I've almost forgotten what it's like. Downstairs, the only thing I do is make baby sounds. When my friends call and talk about what they've been doing and what movies they've seen and ask me what I thought of the new movies, like "Silkwood" or "Frances," I've no idea what they're talking about. All I can talk about is Donald Duck's Christmas or Pippi Longstocking. (*notices the poster between the windows*) What a great poster. . . . I didn't notice it at first. (*a little defensive*) And don't try to talk to me about the theatre.

FRANK

No?

JENNA

(*She sits down on top of the hammer and nails in the chair. Frank notices and grabs the hammer and nails from under her and puts them on the shelf in the entry.*) And it gets so terribly expensive if you need a babysitter. I think the kids are too young. My excursions are mostly taking out the garbage, bringing Sarah to her grandma or buying diapers. That's why it's so incredibly nice to sit here and relax, and not feel like I'm on call the whole time. You've no idea how relaxing this is. I could fall asleep.

KATARINA

We wouldn't mind helping you out now and then, if you need help.

FRANK

With what?

KATARINA

Babysitting.

JENNA

Really? Do you mean it?

KATARINA

Just let us know.

JENNA

(*reluctantly*) Yes, I really will, if it comes up. I mean it would be nice to go out once in a while.

FRANK

I'll take you out. Where do you want to go?

JENNA

Just for a walk. How nice of you, how nice.

KATARINA

Of course.

JENNA

How wonderful. (*Frank has turned on the cassette player. Sinatra is singing "I Didn't Know What Time It Was." Katarina is taking her shoes off and goes into the bedroom.*) My mom loves that one.

FRANK

Katarina thinks he's the worst there is.

JENNA

When I was a little girl . . . at night she used to sing that Frank Sinatra song to me.

FRANK

I think I'd like her.

JENNA

She used to make my bed every morning. She'd feel the sheets and then she'd know what I'd dreamt during the night, she said.

KATARINA

(*by the bedroom door, wearing new shoes*) Let's not talk about our parents. I can't deal with it.

JENNA

Where did you buy those wonderful shoes?

KATARINA

In Old Town.

JENNA

Then I've got to go there.

KATARINA

You can find them anywhere in Rome for half the price.

JENNA

Just to look at them, I mean. (*as if she was all alone*) Ugh, how I'm perspiring. It's pouring out of me. Everything is wet; and I used to be so proud that I never perspired. There used to be something wrong with my glands. But these days I just have to think and I'm all wet. (*to Frank and Katarina*) It has something to do with my pregnancy.

FRANK

It's quite warm in here.

JENNA

The sun is probably beaming on you all day up here. Where's Tomas? (*long pause*) Last night I dropped Wolfgang on the floor while I was nursing him. I dropped him on the floor. He just slid out of my arms.

FRANK

(*tries to be sympathetic*) Oh, oh, how did that happen?

JENNA

I don't know . . . I was asleep . . . that was the second time.

FRANK

So, what would you like to drink? (*Tomas opens the front door.*)

JENNA

Yes, please, something cool. There he is! Tomas! (*loudly*) We are in here! It's Tomas.

TOMAS

It was open.

KATARINA

Tomas! Come in!

TOMAS

Hello.

KATARINA

Finally, hello.

TOMAS

What?

KATARINA

We were wondering what happened to you.

TOMAS

I had to fold the laundry.

KATARINA

Sit down.

JENNA

(*She reaches out with her hand. He touches it as he passes by her.*) You took so long.

SCENE THREE

TOMAS

I had to take the laundry out of the washing machine.

JENNA

I hope you didn't wake him.

KATARINA

(*sitting on the couch*) Come and sit here with me on the couch.

JENNA

Did you turn off the washing machine?

TOMAS

Strange to be in another apartment, and yet it's the same.

FRANK

Not the same. Alike.

TOMAS

What? Yes, that's right.

KATARINA

(*intentionally unfriendly*) Couldn't we turn on some lights, it's so fucking dark up here.

FRANK

Isn't it nice that it's dark.

KATARINA

(*slightly out of control*) If I tell you it's too dark, then shouldn't you be running around turning on lights everywhere? (*to Tomas*) Hello, Tomas.

TOMAS

Hello.

JENNA

He always looks like he just woke up from a nap on the couch. He's a real couch potato.

KATARINA

Hello, hello. (*Frank goes to the kitchen and brings the cassette player with him. Sinatra is still singing.*)

TOMAS

Yes, hello.

KATARINA

Come and sit here! (*intimate*) How are you?

TOMAS

Fine. Really fine.

KATARINA

(*quietly*) I can see that . . . you seem to be really fine.

TOMAS

You too.

KATARINA

Well, maybe . . . well, I dreamt about you last night.

TOMAS

What? About me?

KATARINA

You were big and kind, at least in my dream. It was a wonderful dream.
It's strange about dreams . . . who sneaks in.

JENNA

You did? About what?

KATARINA

Nothing in particular. You've entered my dreams. What are you doing
there? (*Frank turns off the cassette player.*) Did you buy new glasses?

TOMAS

(*takes them off, looks at them*) These? (*massages his eyes*) No, I've had
these for twelve years. Not the same ones. But the same style.

KATARINA

Yes, nice looking. That style suits you.

TOMAS

It's back in fashion again.

KATARINA

(*quickly*) You look good in them.

TOMAS

I never dream. I don't have the time. (*pause*) So, what's happening?

JENNA

We're spending time together.

TOMAS

Aha.

FRANK

(*comes into the room*) How many kids do you have?

KATARINA

How about something to drink?

TOMAS

(*to Jenna*) Why are you so wet?

FRANK

How many kids do you have?

KATARINA

You know.

JENNA

Two. I can't help that I'm so sweaty. It's been like this since the baby was born. (*to Tomas*) You don't have to sleep in the same bed with me.

FRANK

I'm sorry, I mean the little one. Is it a girl?

TOMAS

Who? Wolfgang?

FRANK

Aha. What's his name?

TOMAS

(*very clearly*) Wolfgang.

FRANK

(*surprised*) Not Wolfgang, right?

TOMAS

Yes.

JENNA

After my grandfather . . .

FRANK

Really, and he's already crawling and sitting up and pulling everything down and all that?

TOMAS

(*relaxed, picks up the phone*) No, no, not at all.

FRANK

Maybe he's a little slow. Boys are always a little slower.

KATARINA

Than what?

FRANK

Than girls. Doesn't matter . . . and he's good and healthy?

TOMAS

No, he's sick.

FRANK

Really.

TOMAS

Yes.

JENNA

He's been sick since he was born.

FRANK

You said something about a drink.

TOMAS

He keeps coughing all night long. (*As if he didn't have the strength to say it, he puts the phone down.*)

JENNA

(*thinks he has whooping cough*) Whooping cough. That's nothing dangerous.

FRANK

Poor baby, that's not good when they are that young.

JENNA

It's not dangerous, as long as you keep an eye on them all night long. It was terrible when Sarah had whooping cough.

TOMAS

(*He is looking into the bedroom. The door is open.*) It's so sweet. Somehow it's so touching when they lie there coughing, fighting for air.

FRANK

I guess it's not so good if they fall asleep.

JENNA

No, I had to carry her around half the night. I think I called Tomas twenty times. He was taking a course in Malmo. I didn't know what to do. Finally . . .

KATARINA

How exhausting.

JENNA

It really was. (*pause*) A sleeping child weighs much, much more than it normally does.

KATARINA

I hope she gets well soon. So that you'll be able to sleep.

JENNA

Sarah is fine.

TOMAS

It's Wolfgang.

JENNA

It's Wolfgang who's sick.

TOMAS

It's so touching to hear that hoarse little voice. He almost sounds like Jimmy Durante. (*laughs*)

FRANK

That's a lovely name: Sarah. If I had a daughter her name would be Lena.

KATARINA

No, no, I know so many terrible Sarahs. Yes, I'm sorry. (*smiles at Tomas*)

TOMAS

(*agreeing*) But that's how it is, a name is colored by the people we know.

FRANK

(*We feel how stupid he thinks Tomas is.*) Yes, that's right. (*to Jenna*) That thing you said about sleeping children being much heavier than they normally are, that's interesting.

JENNA

No, I don't know, that's just my experience.

KATARINA

Tomas . . .

TOMAS

Yes.

KATARINA

(*to Frank*) Aren't you going to serve anything?

FRANK

What? Yes, of course. I'm sorry. (*Everyone is looking at him. He pauses.*) What was I thinking?

KATARINA

Wow, you're tense!

FRANK

Me? No, not at all.

KATARINA

Sure you are. Look at your ribcage, it's heaving up and down like a piston. Why the hell don't you relax and behave like a normal person? No one here is going to eat you. . . . Do you hear me, Frank?

FRANK

What?

KATARINA

Calm down.

FRANK

I don't understand what you are talking about. (*Frank sits down on the armrest of Jenna's chair.*) Tea we don't want, but something stronger.

JENNA

(*bends forward and takes a magazine from the table*) Have you seen what a fantastic chair Frank has bought?

FRANK

(*to Katarina*) I don't understand what you're talking about.

TOMAS

Oh my God, is that a chair? (*looks at it for a long time*) It's almost a piece of art.

KATARINA

(*without answering Frank*) It is a piece of art that you can't sit on.

TOMAS

(*Not knowing if he wants to reply, he sits down in the chair.*) Wow, wow, wow, fabulous. How much?

KATARINA

Guess. Three thousand.

TOMAS

Three thousand. Is it true? It can't be true. Not three thousand.

KATARINA

Ask him.

FRANK

(*stands up*) Are you two hungry?

JENNA

Just the opposite, really. (*to Tomas, irritated*) What did you do with the marmalade? You made it yourself.

TOMAS

Oh hell, I forgot it. Do you want me to run down and get it?

JENNA

He's so unbelievably . . .

KATARINA

Tomas? (*Tomas smiles as if he had been complimented.*) There you sit, smiling.

TOMAS

Yes, what am I supposed to do?

KATARINA

About what?

JENNA

Tomas, are you sure you turned the washing machine off?

TOMAS

Yes, yes, yes, at least I think so.

KATARINA

Incredible to see a person who seems so harmonious.

JENNA

(*angrily*) Yes, he's so contented with himself. (*to Frank, who is standing in front of her*) I heard that your mother died. That's terrible.

FRANK

My mother?

JENNA

(*unsure*) Yes, that's what Katarina had said.

FRANK

Why did she say that? (*He smiles, goes to the window, and pauses.*)

JENNA

Didn't she?

KATARINA

She's in the hallway.

JENNA

(*looks at Katarina against her will*) What? What did you say?

KATARINA

She's in a plastic bag, out there, that's where Frank has put her. It's true. There is his little mother. It's true! Isn't she, isn't she, Frank?

FRANK

What?

KATARINA

I'm so sorry, but it sounds . . .

FRANK

(*turns to Katarina*) I can't stand listening to you. What would you like? What would you like to drink?

JENNA

I'm sorry, what did you say? I don't know. Tomas, what do you want?

TOMAS

Yes, anything.

FRANK

(*moves the cocktail cart closer to the couch*) Whiskey, wine? I have a very good white wine called dry pinot.

JENNA

Whiskey would be nice, but then I'll probably fall on my face. If I do, don't bother about me. Just let me stay there.

FRANK

You too, Tomas?

TOMAS

No, I'll stay right here. Sure, whiskey, thank you.

JENNA

(*giggling to herself*) That's what my mother always says. I wish I had the courage to lie under the rug.

TOMAS

(*indifferent*) What does she mean by that? Nothing?

JENNA

You know, to die, of course.

TOMAS

I've never heard her say that.

JENNA

You never heard that?

TOMAS

No.

JENNA

No, of course, why would you? (*aggressively*) You aren't worried sick. You just pretend you are.

FRANK

And what do you want to drink, Katarina?

KATARINA

Gin, if you don't mind.

FRANK

Gin? Already?

KATARINA

Yes, please, if you don't mind.

FRANK

(*like a gentleman, turns to Katarina*) No, why would I mind? (*walks out to the kitchen still whistling the Italian melody*)

TOMAS

(*convincingly*) I do like your mother very much.

JENNA

Strangely enough.

TOMAS

(*even more convincingly*) No, I really do like her.

JENNA

I know you do. Since she thinks that you're the sexiest guy she's ever met.

KATARINA

Oh my . . .

JENNA

The other day she wanted me to divorce you.

TOMAS

What?

JENNA

You heard me.

TOMAS

Why?

KATARINA

Please, let's not talk about our parents. I can't take it. I have my own mother I can't deal with. (*Jenna bends forward and whispers.*) What? (*louder*) What did you say?

JENNA

Is it true that Frank's mother is dead?

KATARINA

We're going to the funeral tomorrow. Yes, of course she's dead. . . . No burial. That glove looks good. (*She means the white protective glove Jenna is wearing on her left hand.*)

JENNA

Yes, I don't understand why it cracks, my skin, I mean. I've had eczema since I was a little girl. I was reading a book about the skin a while ago. There it said that children who aren't loved . . . or . . .

TOMAS

(*at the same time*) Or caressed . . .

JENNA

. . . or caressed will often have problems with their skin, eczema or allergies. But that's not true for me. Not at all. I got so much love when I was young that I was almost hugged to death by everybody.

KATARINA

In Venice I met a man in an outdoor cafe, and he had this beautiful object that looked like a cocktail shaker. It turned out that his mother was dead and had been cremated. And her wish was to be taken to this island . . .

FRANK

Torcello . . .

(*pause*)

KATARINA

Yes . . . and to have her ashes spread over the ocean. He'd taken a boat out and had poured her out over the water. But when he was about to throw the urn in, he thought it was so beautiful. I didn't know there were urns that small. And that was what he was showing me. He was sitting there with it on top of the cafe table as if he was about to shake a cocktail. (*Everyone is laughing, even if they didn't find it funny, except Frank. Katarina speaks to Frank when she is done laughing.*) Isn't that a funny one?

FRANK

Sure. A hell of a funny story.

KATARINA

(*to Tomas*) He doesn't laugh . . . doesn't dare.

TOMAS

(*who doesn't know her intention*) Why not?

KATARINA

Where's my drink? (*Frank ignores her.*)

TOMAS

That's quite a story.

KATARINA

Then he discovered . . .

FRANK

Cheers! (*to Jenna*)

JENNA

I guess we'll never get to Venice.

KATARINA

(*to Frank, in a mean way*) Then he discovered what an incredible power of attraction he had on little girls on the beach, so then he lost interest in the urn. Right, Frank?

FRANK

I don't think I heard what you were saying. Cheers! (*to Tomas*)

KATARINA

Don't bother with what I'm saying.

FRANK

What have you been saying?

KATARINA

Nothing . . . kiss, kiss. (*takes his hand and holds it lovingly*) Do you say kiss, kiss too?

JENNA

Kiss?

KATARINA

When you talk on the phone? (*Jenna shakes her head.*) I get really worried . . . then there's something wrong, if we don't say kiss, kiss before we hang up. Right, Frank? (*Frank nods and smells his hand. It smells of her.*)

TOMAS

What great whiskey.

KATARINA

I wait to the last moment . . . and if he doesn't say kiss, kiss but hangs up just like that, I don't feel good.

FRANK

So, you like it?

KATARINA

We've got to say kiss, kiss until we die.

TOMAS

Really good, what kind is it?

KATARINA

Where's my gin?

JENNA

I think all whiskey tastes the same.

TOMAS

No, not at all.

JENNA

Okay, then. (*pause*) Is it true? Your mom . . .

FRANK

I could make some espresso. My mom!

JENNA

Is she really in a plastic bag out there in the hallway?

FRANK

Yes.

JENNA

She shouldn't be out there, should she?

FRANK

Buried, but not dead. As they say. No, cremated, but not dead.

JENNA

Isn't that strange?

FRANK

What?

JENNA

But you aren't going to keep her there?

FRANK

My brother and his wife will be here tomorrow and then we're going out to the cemetery to bury her there. (*Frank bends down and listens to the phone.*) Me and my brother and his wife.

KATARINA

(*takes a cigarette from Frank's breast pocket*) Sounds like I'm not going.

FRANK

They sent her to me from the funeral home in a little package. I went to the post office and picked her up. She was so small, so dainty. Do you want to see? (*Frank goes to the hallway.*)

JENNA

Ugh, no thanks. (*keeps on rolling her skirt up her thigh*)

FRANK

Just some ashes. (*pause*)

KATARINA

This Sunday I'm going to the country to visit my mother.

FRANK

How nice.

KATARINA

My God. (*She bends forward, lets Tomas, who stands up, light her cigar-ette, and says "thank you" before he does it. Frank puts the plastic bag in front of the bathroom door.*)

FRANK

Why do you always cut off the filter like that?

KATARINA

I really have to. . . . What did you say?

FRANK

(*sits down next to Katarina on the couch*) You see, this is what I said, why do you cut the filter off your filter cigarette? Why do you buy filter cigarettes when you keep cutting off the filters? I don't understand it. Why do you do it?

KATARINA

Does one have to understand everything one does?

JENNA

(*holding her breasts*) Wow, it's that time again.

TOMAS

What is it?

JENNA

I'm going crazy. (*pause*) Do you think it's okay for me to drink strong liquor when I'm nursing? (*touches her breasts*) It's pouring.

FRANK

Is it pouring?

JENNA

Yes, wow, oh my. (*silence*)

FRANK

How does it feel?

JENNA

I have to go to the bathroom.

FRANK

Yes, of course. (*stands up*) You know where it is.

JENNA

(*stares pleadingly at Tomas who gives off a grunt*) What did you say?

TOMAS

No, nothing. Don't be difficult now.

JENNA

Oh no, I won't be difficult, I'll just crawl out there. (*She goes to the bathroom and keeps herself pressed to the wall just to get away from the urn. Frank sits down.*)

TOMAS

What did she mean by that?

FRANK

How wonderful.

KATARINA

What's so wonderful?

FRANK

A woman with breasts that are pouring and everything. What do you think, Tomas?

TOMAS

(*He looks as if he thought it rather unpleasant, as if he experienced Jenna as weak and demanding.*) It takes time.

FRANK

What?

TOMAS

Well, before they look good again.

KATARINA

Good? . . . What do you mean by that?

TOMAS

Before they're back again, before they've come back and the body has started to function normally. I don't know how to say it. We aren't having any more kids. (*not unfriendly*) I just have to lie down next to her and she gets pregnant.

(*noise from the bathroom*)

JENNA

Ouch!

TOMAS

(*like a child*) What the hell is she doing?

FRANK

(*wants to get up*) Oh fuck, there's a hell of a lot of broken glass in there. Katarina went a little crazy before.

KATARINA

Shut up.

JENNA

(*miserable*) Tomas, Tomas!

TOMAS

Yes, what's wrong?

JENNA

(*pause*) Can't you come here and help me?

FRANK

So answer her then.

TOMAS

What do you want?

JENNA

Tomas! Tomas!

TOMAS

Yeees!

JENNA

Why don't you come, when I'm calling you?

TOMAS

My God, now what? This is really silly. (*He doesn't want to but is forced to stand up, goes to her, and puts his glasses on the floor.*)

KATARINA

What? (*Frank is neutral, doesn't answer.*) You're looking at me as if I were an animal.

FRANK

You are.

KATARINA

Really.

FRANK

A little cockroach. (*smiles*)

TOMAS

(*comes in, stops by the bathroom door*) She has soiled her blouse. What the hell can I do about that? Do you have something I can borrow to give her? Anything.

KATARINA

I don't think so. Do you want me to look? (*She stands up, is very irritated, goes to the bedroom, comes back with a very big woolen sweater, and throws it to Tomas.*) Well, this is the only thing I have. Otherwise you'll have to run downstairs and find something.

(*pause*)

TOMAS

No, this is okay. (*He throws the sweater to Jenna through the half-closed door, picks up his glass, drinks, and looks at what's left in his glass.*) Well, well, well.

FRANK

What did you say?

TOMAS

Well, well, well.

FRANK

Aha . . . how's it going?

TOMAS

You know how it is.

FRANK

No.

TOMAS

You know, mostly work and then home to eat, and then putting the kids to bed.

FRANK

(*far away in his thoughts*) There's no time for anything.

(*Katarina goes to the kitchen for some white wine.*)

TOMAS

(*more concentrated on what Katarina is doing*) I guess that's enough. I play a little tennis.

FRANK

Tennis? Tennis?

TOMAS

Yes, and you?

FRANK

Well, you know . . . but Tomas, why don't we start to play tennis together, you and me, once a week? (*whistles*) What do say?

TOMAS

You and me?

FRANK

Yes, what do you say?

TOMAS

No, I already have someone I play with.

FRANK

You have? Tennis?

TOMAS

Yes, exactly.

FRANK

Not squash?

TOMAS

No, tennis. What do you do?

FRANK

Me?

TOMAS

What do you do? Intellectual bodybuilding? (*Frank laughs and is humming.*) Tell me.

FRANK

(*thinking*) Yea, what do I do? I really try to run six miles every morning.

TOMAS

Where?

FRANK

Where?

TOMAS

Yes.

FRANK

Around and around . . . the whole time . . . (*Katarina comes into the living room.*) Are you angry?

TOMAS

No.

FRANK

You sounded angry. Are you sure?

TOMAS

No, I'm not.

KATARINA

Do you know what you're humming?

FRANK

What? . . . No, no idea.

KATARINA

That song, your Italian whore that you fucked in the toilet at Orly Airport.

FRANK

Oh hell, I didn't think that was what I was whistling.

KATARINA

You weren't whistling. You were humming.

FRANK

It wasn't Orly. (*smiles*)

KATARINA

(*pause*) Where's Jenna?

FRANK

She's curled up in the sandbox. (*to Tomas*) Are you sure you aren't angry?

TOMAS

Yes.

FRANK

So, I didn't upset you, did I?

TOMAS

(*friendly, sits on the couch*) No, you couldn't.

FRANK

Okay, good.

KATARINA

(*suddenly screams*) Giiiiin!

FRANK

What did you say?

KATARINA

Aren't we getting any more to drink?

FRANK

(*stands up*) Maybe so. Tomas, do you want another one?

TOMAS

Yes, why not.

FRANK

So, what do you want? Whiskey? Gin?

TOMAS

Whatever.

FRANK

(*goes to the cocktail cart*) That's what you'll get then.

KATARINA

Frank? Frank?

FRANK

Yes, Katarina, what do you want now?

KATARINA

Well . . . mmm . . . mmm, I'd love something to eat, since you're going to the kitchen anyway. Why don't you bring us something when you come back? (*Frank doesn't know what to do and snaps his fingers. Tomas stands up, goes to the window, and gives his empty glass to Frank.*) Darling. (*A passenger plane, fully lit, is passing quickly, soundlessly outside the window in the evening sky.*)

FRANK

What did you say? (*pours something into Tomas's glass.*)

KATARINA

(*smiles encouragingly*) Darling. (*short pause*)

SCENE FOUR

(*Frank gives Tomas the glass and walks into the bedroom.*)

KATARINA

(*gives Frank an amused look*) Oh my, he's mad . . . wow, wow, wow . . . this is going to be fun. (*smiles at Tomas*) Hello . . . hello, is that you?

TOMAS

Yes, of course it's me.

KATARINA

(*She looks at him. He looks at her, but stops after a while. They look at each other. Tomas sits down in the couch again.*) Oh my, he's angry. Do you hear all the noise he's making? (*Katarina goes behind the couch, sits on the edge and puts her hand on it.*)

TOMAS

(*He puts his hand on hers. They quickly pull their hands back.*) Sorry . . . sorry, my fault. (*He scratches his hand, a habit of his.*)

KATARINA

I didn't experience it as a fault.

TOMAS

No . . . what?

KATARINA

You happened to touch my hand . . . what were you going to say?

TOMAS

Just resting it on the couch.

KATARINA

Your hand?

TOMAS

Yes?

KATARINA

So do it then. (*Tomas again happens to touch her hand. Katarina bends backwards, smelling her hand on the side of her shoulder, almost subconsciously. Her need for scents is very strong and unassailable. She sneezes.*) You shouldn't wear that kind of cologne, it's much too common. You smell just like my mom. You should find a different kind.

TOMAS

What kind? (*caresses Katarina's hand*)

KATARINA

(*pulls her hand away*) I get so tired.

TOMAS

Really.

KATARINA

What would you say if you were awakened every morning by someone who's throwing a load of crap at you, a whole load of crap in your face? (*Katarina goes to the window.*)

TOMAS

Nice looking dress.

KATARINA

You think so?

TOMAS

Yes. Black looks good on you.

KATARINA

I like black.

TOMAS

(*unsure*) Yes, I do too.

KATARINA

You do? (*pause*) In Italy it isn't unusual to dress up, to look elegant, the way it is here; there, even the poorest worker has a dark suit and a pair of great looking shoes. I want to look elegant. I like your shirt. . . . (*Katarina sits on the couch; she sneezes.*) My mom . . . you'd like my mom. (*sniffs, sneezes*)

TOMAS

Your mom?

KATARINA

You smell just like her. Strange.

TOMAS

Maybe we use the same cologne. (*Frank comes back from the bedroom.*)

FRANK

What are you two talking about?

KATARINA

(*friendly*) You.

FRANK

Didn't anyone wonder where Jenna went? (*He goes to the bathroom, knocks on the door and comes back with her.*)

JENNA

(*in the strong light, blinking*) I'm sorry . . . I almost fell asleep . . . I feel sick to my stomach.

FRANK

Come and sit here with me.

JENNA

Tomas, I said that I feel sick. . . .

TOMAS

What did you say? . . . You do, darling? (*pause*) Do you feel sick to your stomach?

JENNA

Forget it! Am I disturbing . . .?

TOMAS

Who?

JENNA

I don't mean you. If that's what you think.

TOMAS

No, I guess you don't.

FRANK

(*brings Jenna to the easy chair*) Yes, you look very pale.

KATARINA

Drink a little whiskey.

JENNA

(*to Frank*) It's been like this for almost a whole year. It's so depressing, I'm sorry. (*pause*) I remember when I was pregnant with Wolfgang and took Sarah to daycare. . . .

KATARINA

Sarah is the daughter of Jenna and Tomas.

JENNA

She was four then. Now she's almost five. She is with her grandma.

TOMAS

Are you trying to tell us something? You started to say something.

JENNA

I've nothing to say. I might as well go home. (*in an empty tone of voice*) I've nothing to say. Nothing. I might as well . . .

TOMAS

(*nonchalantly*) What?

JENNA

Keep my mouth shut.

FRANK

Please tell us.

JENNA

What? . . . Why? It wasn't anything special. It will just sound silly. I don't want to look like a fool.

FRANK

You aren't silly. Not at all. Now tell us.

JENNA

It's not funny. . . . It was just something that happened in my second
month, when I was pregnant. (*She falls silent, then tells the story without
emotion and without caring if anyone is listening or not.*) I felt sick and I
was throwing up almost every morning. On the bus, I tried to hold it back
so that I wouldn't throw up until I got to the bed of tulips outside Sarah's
daycare, and one morning she pointed to the other flowerbed and said . . .

TOMAS

(*at the same time*) That one too, Mommy.

JENNA

That one too, Mommy. I knew it wasn't very funny.

FRANK

(*He laughs loudly, a laugh that never seems to end, and notices they are
all looking at him.*) Please excuse the way I laugh. (*again laughs just as
loudly*) I know what I sound like. (*to Jenna*) That was goddamn funny.
Now I've got to take a leak. (*He goes to the bathroom. They all sit in
silence, and are forced to listen since he doesn't shut the door.*)

JENNA

(*quietly, tenderly*) Aren't you going to have any children?

KATARINA

(*also quietly*) No . . . no.

FRANK

(*is coming back, friendly*) Anyone for another drink?

JENNA

What time is it?

FRANK

You look very tired, Jenna. . . . Do you want to lie down for a little
while? (*to Tomas*) Look at her . . .

(*Jenna stands up and staggers over to Tomas.*)

TOMAS

(*quickly gets up from the couch and stands behind it.*) Is it time to throw up again?

FRANK

Maybe you better lie down?

JENNA

(*mimics Tomas*) Is it time to throw up again? (*She shakes her head. Frank brings Jenna to lie down on the couch.*)

KATARINA

Yes, isn't that going to be nice for you?

FRANK

(*looks at her.*) Me? . . . What?

KATARINA

Tomorrow, when you don't have to be with me. (*now standing, goes to the table*)

FRANK

(*to himself*) Yes, that's right. You're right. (*to Jenna*) Jenna, do you want a pillow? . . . You should lie down. (*sits down on the couch*)

FRANK

(*to Tomas*) Have you seen any good films lately?

JENNA

No.

TOMAS

I'm thinking of getting a video player, maybe rent one. I don't know.

JENNA

(*quietly, with strong intensity*) Never in my life. Never. Do you hear me. We aren't getting any video player. We are not having a video player. I'll break it, I tell you. It's horrible. Horrible! Do you really think I want to watch those things . . . whatever it is . . . people being torn apart . . . do you think I want that . . . do you?!

TOMAS

(after a long while) Yes . . . no . . .

JENNA

Do you think I'm longing for that? (*pause*) Is that what you think? (*very strong, straight out*) We are not going to have a video player.

FRANK

No?

JENNA

Then you might as well murder the kids. And me too. Then you can sit there with your video all night long.

TOMAS

But I love watching movies. . . . (*trying to repair something*) I don't understand. . . . It's not at all because I want to watch those kinds of . . . I've always loved . . .

JENNA

(*furious*) Don't you hear what I'm saying? If you buy a video player I'll throw it out the window!

TOMAS

(*laughing in spite of his anger*) I guess this is of no interest to Katarina and Frank.

JENNA

You heard me. If you absolutely have to watch people go at each other like wild animals, you'll have to do that some other place, but not in our home.

KATARINA

(*She interrupts her loudly, takes the whiskey bottle, and fills the glasses.*) Yes, I'd like to go to a movie. . . . Is there a special one you'd like to see?

FRANK

(*smiles as if they were alone*) Nooo . . . thinking of . . . "The Night Porter."

JENNA

I'll throw it out the window.

KATARINA

We already saw it.

FRANK

Not me. (*to Jenna*) Did you see "The Night Porter"?

JENNA

(*very angry*) Why do you ask, when you know I haven't been to the movies for three years?!

TOMAS

(*with an uneasy smile*) Well, there seems to be no lack of martyrs in here.

KATARINA

Bullshit! Of course we've seen it . . .

JENNA

What are you talking about?

KATARINA

You and me, we did, we really did . . .

FRANK

Not me.

KATARINA

Of course we did!

JENNA

(*staring angrily at Tomas*) I heard what you said.

KATARINA

Don't you remember?

FRANK

I know what you're doing . . .

TOMAS

It was meant as a . . .

FRANK

I said I know what you're doing. Do you think I'm impressed?

JENNA

Don't belittle yourself, Tomas.

FRANK

No, I said.

JENNA

Don't try to make yourself smaller . . .

KATARINA

Of course you did.

JENNA

Tomas, don't try to make yourself smaller than you are . . .

KATARINA

Sure you did.

JENNA

Dear Tomas, don't try to . . .

FRANK

I say no.

JENNA

Then there won't be much left.

KATARINA

Of course you did! . . . It wasn't "The Night Porter" . . . or was it "The Night Porter"?

TOMAS

What do you mean by that? (*pause*)

JENNA

I'm not crazy.

FRANK

Of course you aren't.

KATARINA

(*almost howling*) What fucking movie was it?

FRANK

I don't know.

JENNA

Do you hear me?

KATARINA

(*still loudly*) You don't know? Why don't you know?

FRANK

How the hell am I supposed to remember all the movies you've seen.

KATARINA

Maybe because you saw it with me.

FRANK

(*He takes the glass in which Katarina has poured whiskey.*) *Skoal*, Jenna.

JENNA

(*Jenna doesn't move.*) We aren't having any VCR.

FRANK

Skoal, Jenna.

KATARINA

Tomas!

TOMAS

Yes . . . I'm here.

KATARINA

(*Katarina brings Tomas a big glass, then goes back to the table and pours herself an even bigger glass, very exaggerated.*) *Skooooaaal*, Tomas.

JENNA

So drink, then. (*pause*) Drink. (*pause*) Drink when they tell you to. (*pause*) Look, he's drinking. Drink more. Keep on drinking. (*pause*)

TOMAS

(*slightly embarrassed*) No . . . I haven't been to the movies for quite a while. . . . When my buddies ask me if I've seen "Frances" or "Star

Wars" . . . (*embarrassed laughter*) I've only seen Donald Duck and
Mickey Mouse . . .

JENNA

(*at the same time*) . . . or Bambi.

TOMAS

It makes you feel like a fool.

JENNA

Fine. I already explained our life to Katarina and Frank long before you
came.

TOMAS

Really, well sorry . . . but you really do start to feel a little . . . what is it
called? . . .

FRANK

Excited?

TOMAS

What? (*as if he finally had someone to fight with*) What did you say?
What the hell did you say?

FRANK

Excited?

TOMAS

No, that's not it.

FRANK

I didn't? Katarina? Wasn't that what I said?

JENNA

Don't you think you should go downstairs and check on Wolfgang?

TOMAS

Don't you try to stick your nose in this. (*No one speaks. He picks up the
phone and listens.*) Why should I? There isn't even a peep.

JENNA

Maybe he's dead.

TOMAS

Quiet as a grave. Listen yourself.

JENNA

Then he'll wake up soon. . . . (*to Katarina*) Sure, once he gave me a night out by myself, and told me to run out to a movie. Maybe there was something he wanted to do by himself at home.

TOMAS

Why do you say things like that? "Gave you a night out?" . . . Jenna, little Jenna . . . Jenna. (*pleading*) It's not only because of Wolfgang that you don't go out.

JENNA

Do you think I'm having fun! Is that what you think?

TOMAS

But little Jenna . . .

JENNA

Is that what you think! Is that what you think!

TOMAS

What?

JENNA

Don't you think I'd like to get out of the house sometimes, just go out by myself? All by myself! . . . Don't you think I'd like to see a play sometime or some real people? Fuck, I don't even know what people look like any more! And don't call me "little Jenna." I'm never out of the house. . . . I won't tell you where I'm going. I'm not going to tell you. No one will know. (*Katarina goes to the bathroom.*) Don't you hear what I'm saying? . . . (*Frank stands up then goes to the window.*) Don't just stand there. . . . You've got to go downstairs and look at him. It's your turn.

TOMAS

Sure . . . of course.

JENNA

So go then!

TOMAS

What?

JENNA

I told you to go downstairs . . . go down and see if he's breathing. You know he has the whooping cough, don't you? . . . And I'll stay here and talk to . . .

TOMAS

Right now? Why? Why now? . . . I'll go down there when he needs to be fed.

JENNA

Now, I said.

TOMAS

Dear Jenna, try to calm down a little.

JENNA

I want you to go downstairs right now! Tomas, right now!

FRANK

Take it easy.

JENNA

Tomas, right now!

TOMAS

Yeah, yeah, what the hell, I'm going. I'm going. Whatever you want. I'm leaving right now. (*goes out to the hallway*)

JENNA

(*almost desperate*) Go. Just go.

TOMAS

I am, I'm going. (*leaves*)

JENNA

(*helpless*) He doesn't love me. He never did. (*as if she doesn't know what she is saying*) That's why I get pregnant all the time. (*She calms down. We see that she is a very good person, nice and straightforward.*)

FRANK

(*goes over to Jenna*) How are you feeling?

JENNA

(*after a long pause*) Fine, I think, I think you're horrible. Both of you.

FRANK

I think so too. (*Jenna stands up and goes towards the hallway.*) Where are you going? Are you going downstairs too? Why are you leaving? Don't go. Don't go.

JENNA

I want to see what he's doing.

FRANK

(*follows her*) Don't go.

SCENE FIVE

FRANK

Don't go.

JENNA

I want to see what he's doing.

FRANK

(*follows her*) Don't go!

(*Jenna leaves. Katarina is coming out of the bathroom door.*)

KATARINA

What's going on?

FRANK

They were going downstairs to check on their kid, Wolfgang, I guess? (*Katarina walks towards the chair.*)

KATARINA

What the hell is this running up and down. You invited them. I guess they'll be back?

FRANK

(*He turns on the radio in the kitchen. Italian classical music is heard.*) If you say so.

KATARINA

His eye glasses are over there.

FRANK

I think you're right. . . . If you want to come back to a place, you would probably leave something behind. (*Frank smiles and sits down behind Katarina.*)

KATARINA

Are you drunk?

FRANK

No, I'm sober. Very sober. (*quietly*) I'm just smiling.

KATARINA

What's that scent you are wearing? (*without interest*) It smells good.

FRANK

Nino Cerutti.

KATARINA

Everything seems to have been made in Italy these days. Gucci shoes. Italian aftershave. Your cigarettes. The chair . . . (*Katarina sits down on top of Tomas's glasses.*) So, are you still seeing her?

FRANK

No. Better not to have it but to dream about it, than having it and not dream about it. Nino Cerutti really isn't Italian.

KATARINA

Of course it is. It's one of the most famous Italian brands.

FRANK

(*shrugs*) Even though it's French.

KATARINA

It's not. Absolutely not. It's typically Italian. Go and get the bottle and you'll see.

FRANK

I will. (*He picks up the bottle from the table.*)

KATARINA

The first time I lived alone in Rome I was only fourteen, so I went through my Italian neurosis a long time ago. (*puts on Tomas's glasses*)

FRANK

(*He comes back and removes Tomas's glasses from Katarina.*) Look, Nino Cerutti *pour homme* . . . eight-five percent volume, one hundred milliliters, three-point-three fluid ounces, Paris. Do you see that? Paris? *Pour homme*. Paris is still situated in France. . . . Okay? Okay? Okay?

KATARINA

Is it expensive?

FRANK

Don't even fucking go there. Is it Italian or French?

KATARINA

Now that they've left, I hear that you are still you.

FRANK

So, it's not Italian then. Good.

KATARINA

It probably is.

FRANK

What the hell are you talking about!

KATARINA

Most brands are registered in a different country than where they were originally made. I can give you at least twenty examples.

FRANK

I don't give a damn. (*suddenly furious*) This one is not Italian! It's not Italian!

KATARINA

But all the others are. Raffi Linea Uomo is Italian. Domus is an Italian magazine. (*to herself*) That music that you're playing is Italian.

FRANK

Well, so what?

KATARINA

It's so . . . depressing. (*pause*) Why do you have to be like this?

FRANK

I have to.

KATARINA

(*in a way meant to hurt him*) It doesn't matter any longer. I've been through this too many times. It doesn't matter. You can't hurt me any longer, Frank. . . . (*Frank goes to the kitchen, turns off the radio, and stands in the doorway holding Tomas's glasses.*) What are they doing? Are they making another baby? . . . Have you ever seen their apartment? What a terrible place.

FRANK

I'll have to remember to say "good night" to Mom before I go to bed. . . . I think I'll let her sleep where you usually sleep.

KATARINA

I guess she always did. (*smiles*) Be careful not to get on top of her.

FRANK

(*Still standing wearing the glasses, he looks at her, takes them off, puts them back on, then speaks, almost tenderly.*) You look old, Katarina . . . Goddamn old. You look terrible. Just look at those droopy lines around your mouth, lines you probably don't think you have to hide any longer. Seeing them makes for a very unpleasant . . . experience.

KATARINA

Well, there are so many other things about me that are so much more attractive and . . . deep. Why do you keep doing this?

FRANK

You don't know? (*He takes off the glasses, puts them in his breast pocket, and walks towards Katarina.*) So, you really don't know why? All, and I mean all, alcoholism is caused by hatred towards women.

KATARINA

Really. What does that have to do with this? (*Katarina looks at him as if he was crazy.*)

FRANK

That's how it is.

KATARINA

Women's alcoholism as well?

FRANK

(*a forced smile*) Of course. (*The smile gets bigger.*) You keep fighting all the time. All you want to do is win.

KATARINA

Me?

FRANK

Yes, you!

KATARINA

What do I want to win? I just want to feel good.

FRANK

"I've had enough," you said.

KATARINA

That's true.

FRANK

Of what? You'll never have enough.

KATARINA

Of you.

FRANK

I understand that, but do you have to tell our neighbors?

KATARINA

(*without getting up*) I can't take it, no one would be able to take it. . . . Women want . . .

FRANK

Do you like Jenna? Do you like her? What were you going to say?

KATARINA

Women want men who are seeking . . .

FRANK

What?

KATARINA

Women want men who are seeking . . .

FRANK

Women have no cunt.

KATARINA

. . . comfort from them . . . who say, "I need you . . . hold me . . . comfort me."

FRANK

Did you hear me? It's women who have no cunt. Comfort me, why?

KATARINA

(*very serious*) That's what you don't understand and what I can't explain to you.

FRANK

(*goes to the table*) I'm sorry . . . I'm so sorry.

KATARINA

But you . . . you can't . . . you aren't like that . . . not you . . . you always put up a wall around you . . . (*Frank coughs.*) And don't tell me that you aren't incredibly upset. . . . (*He coughs again, drinks, then sits on the couch.*) You can't do anything about the way you hold your head or the way you cough or whatever, when you are upset, and right now it's very bad. (*very hurt*) But you'd never say, "Katarina, please hold me, help me, I need to cry, I need you . . . I feel so lonely and abandoned," would you? (*silence*) You see . . . you can't say it . . . not even now, that your mother is dead, can you come to me. . . . I need a man who doesn't have such self control. . . . I want someone who can fall apart. . . . I want a . . . normal man.

FRANK

Tonight?

KATARINA

(*Suddenly there is a chill in the room.*) Okay.

FRANK

(*He lies down on the couch.*) Okay? . . . I want some coffee. (*pause*)

KATARINA

I don't want to fight with you anymore. . . . You won . . . be my guest. You're the best one. I'm the worst. You're the winner. I'm the looser. You're much more intelligent than I am. You're much better at handling money than I am. Your cunt is much lovelier than mine. And so on, and so on, and so on. . . . I don't care. I don't care about anything.

FRANK

Do you want some coffee? Not espresso, right?

KATARINA

No . . .

FRANK

(*He gets up from the couch.*) I want coffee. I think I'll have a big cup of latte. Do you want a cup of latte too, with dark chocolate flakes on top? I feel like I'm on vacation. It's that kind of mood. The last day on some kind of beach, an afternoon drink. You feel tired and there's a pain in your heart. (*Frank goes to the kitchen.*)

KATARINA

(*Furious that he might have slipped out of her hold, she runs after him and kicks him.*) You're crazy! You're a sadist!

FRANK

(*calmly*) What are you doing?

KATARINA

Kicking you.

FRANK

(*He closes the kitchen door. They look at each other through the glass in the door.*) Yes, I can feel it. Cut that out.

KATARINA

Frank, have you noticed that you're sick? . . . Frank, dear Frank . . . I want to reach you! You're crazy! You're just laughing! What am I to do? (*Frank lets go of the doorknob. Katarina comes into the kitchen and closes the door behind her.*)

FRANK

(*He picks up a crystal vase filled with water and pours it over her head. She is standing still and lets it happen.*) Please do not create any scenes tonight . . . you know what I mean. No theatre. No erotic theatre. Tonight I don't want you to run around playing dog without a master. (*Katarina gets away, her skirt rips, and she sinks down on the floor, her hair all wet.*) Do you hear what I'm saying?

KATARINA

Thank you.

FRANK

Do you hear me?

KATARINA

(*very calmly*) Dear Frank, thank you!

FRANK

Take it easy now.

KATARINA

It's fine.

FRANK

Good.

KATARINA

Believe me. (*There is a long pause. Katarina stands up and falls through the kitchen door. Glass is everywhere. During the continued dialogue there is blood dripping everywhere, without them noticing anything, as if time didn't exist.*)

FRANK

(*still holding the crystal vase*) What's going on? . . . Are you going crazy?

KATARINA

(*on her knees in the hallway*) I don't give a damn about you. . . . I don't give a damn about you any longer. . . . You aren't a human being. . . . You are . . . fucking mental. . . .

FRANK

Okay, okay, now go into the bedroom and change clothes.

KATARINA

(*without fear of being hit*) I'm just so incredibly grateful that I met you, so that I had someone else to think about during the first five years after I had divorced David, who is the love of my life, and whom I'll never get over. I want you to know that, that you've helped me many times, entertained me, one could say. Otherwise I would have gone mad from sorrow. I was almost insane when we first met, but then I thought that I could always amuse myself with you for the time being. I thought . . .

FRANK

(*interrupts*) Okay. Okay. Say whatever you want. You can leave now or leave in the morning. But none of your shit, okay?

KATARINA

(*touches her ripped dress, very calmly*) It cost me three hundred dollars. I want it back.

FRANK

Oh yes, you'll get everything back, as long as you do what I say.

KATARINA

(*She stands up, disgusted.*) I wonder what it feels like . . . to be like you, with your head between your legs. I'll be damned if I can't make you break down.

FRANK

But first go and change your clothes.

KATARINA

I'll get you to break down.

FRANK

You will?

KATARINA

Yes, I will. I usually get what I want.

FRANK

You know, Katarina, I've finally discovered that it's possible to fuck because you love someone and fuck without loving someone; and I want to say . . . that to fuck you without feeling love, which is what I've done these last weeks, is a terrible experience—it's like fucking a corpse.

KATARINA

(*walks towards the chair*) Believe me, that is what you've been doing.

FRANK

One thing I'll swear to: If you existed, I'd kill you.

KATARINA

A corpse. Now I'm going to start living. Now I feel like being alive again while making love. I'm not going to change my clothes. (*sits on the couch*) I'm going to sit here on the couch and show them how you're treating me.

FRANK

You do that. . . . (*very threatening, walks towards her, puts the crystal vase on the table*) But just don't start any of your shit. Not tonight.

TOMAS

(*from the front door*) Did I put my glasses here somewhere?

SCENE SIX

FRANK

Did you bring the marmalade?

TOMAS

Did I put my glasses here somewhere?

FRANK

Hello there, there you are. (*Tomas first looks in the sofa, then on the table, then in the bathroom, and back in the living room.*) Look at this mess. Who's been here, a whore?

TOMAS
(*is standing behind Frank*) What did you say?

FRANK
A whore. How's Ludwig?

TOMAS
Who's Ludwig?

FRANK
Do I really have to tell you who your son is?

TOMAS
You mean Wolfgang. He has the hiccups.

FRANK
Don't stand there breathing down my neck.

TOMAS
A whore?

FRANK
Maybe . . . what are you looking for?

TOMAS
My glasses.

FRANK
Your glasses?

TOMAS
Yes, didn't I put them here somewhere before I went downstairs?

FRANK
Did you really? You didn't go downstairs, did you?

TOMAS
Here somewhere.

FRANK
Well, only you know where they are.

TOMAS

(*to Katarina who goes to the kitchen*) Did you see them?

FRANK

Katarina?

TOMAS

I'm the one asking, not you.

FRANK

(*sits on the couch*) No, that's what I said, I said "Katarina."

TOMAS

Is she coming back?

FRANK

That's a good question. I've seen them.

TOMAS

Where?

FRANK

(*smiles*) Earlier, when you were wearing them. After that they've completely fallen out of my memory. Everything's falling. Let it fall. (*about
to get up*) I hope I'm not sitting on them.

TOMAS

(*is looking in the chair*) No, they aren't here. . . . No, I didn't put them
here.

FRANK

No? Why don't you bring Katarina with you to look in the bedroom?

(*Katarina comes into the room holding a frying pan. She hits Frank in
the head.*)

TOMAS

(*turns to them*) What the hell?

(*Katarina leaves. She goes into the bathroom.*)

FRANK

(*to Tomas*) What did you say?

TOMAS

(*walks towards the front door*) Nothing.

FRANK

You see, I've got something, she needs fucking badly; and, you see, I'm not going to give it to her. . . . Is it you or me with the foot odor? (*Frank gets up and goes to the table. He has a headache.*) We've the same shirt. (*pause*) We've the same shirt.

TOMAS

We do?

FRANK

Don't we? But you're wearing a tie. . . . Do you have two ties? I'll put mine on when you're gone.

TOMAS

I'm not leaving.

FRANK

No? How nice. Have you been fighting? (*pause*) That's sad. When that happens . . . Tomas?

TOMAS

What?

FRANK

No, I was just wondering what it is you're looking for. (*Tomas is looking at the magazines on the plastic table.*) That's an interesting magazine, the one you have in your hand—*Abitare*. There's a big story . . . about English homes, in the middle. It almost opens there by itself; just put it down and let it open up by itself. . . . That one you can look at . . . but don't touch the others . . . don't touch those, I said. (*pause*) Don't you hear what I'm telling you? I said, don't touch them! Don't fucking touch them, I said!

TOMAS

What? What are you saying?

FRANK

Don't fucking touch those magazines! Leave them there.

TOMAS

I'm just picking them up.

FRANK

That's how you see it, yes. But that's not how I see it. (*pause*) Are you crazy?

TOMAS

Then I'll put them down.

FRANK

Why? (*pause*) Why don't you sit down instead and I'll give you a drink? (*Tomas shakes his head.*) Don't be silly now . . . (*pause*) You're a teacher, aren't you?

TOMAS

A teacher?

FRANK

And you're paranoid and you don't make it easy for yourself. No, I understand . . . there's something I've been thinking about. When we were little, you and me, the first thing people asked was, "What are you going to be when you grow up?" . . . Do you remember? (*pause*) Of course you do. (*pause*) Do you really mean that no one ever asked you what you wanted to be when you grow up? . . . How strange . . . that's just what I mean. It doesn't work anymore. That's a question you can't ask kids any more. . . . Isn't that frightening . . . if you think about it? Sit down . . . (*gives Tomas a glass, he sits down in the chair*) . . . and I'll tell you about my cousin Maria. Do you want me to tell you about my cousin Maria? Do you want to know who she is? Do you want to know what she means to me? . . . When I was seven she seduced me in our attic. (*sits on the table*) Yes . . . when she pulled down the foreskin on my prick I thought my head would fall off. I became filled with panic. Ran out in the yard and threw myself on my bike and kept biking around the block five, six times. . . . She was also seven. After that we were together every summer. . . . She lived in the city, but in the summer she was with us in the country . . . and we were together, used to sneak up and . . . and we fucked . . . it was thrilling. . . . I'll never forget her little noises, how proud I felt. But the summer she turned fourteen and came to us as usual . . . then she had developed breasts . . . and when all the grownups had gone to bed I knocked on her door and wanted to come in, and she did let me in, and I don't know what we were talking about . . . but when I stood behind her and tried to caress her breasts—breasts I had looked at all day long—she got furious, turned around and hit me and asked what I was doing. . . . I don't think I understood what she was saying, but tried again, to touch them, but she'd become someone else, she'd become vile and rotten, but I took revenge. I sold her to my buddies, they fucked her, five of them in a big hole in the ground behind a factory. . . . Do you know what that chair smells like when it's raining? . . . Human beings. Humans. Human beings.

TOMAS

I guess human beings sit in it.

FRANK

(*stands up*) I never do. Haven't you noticed that I never sit in that chair? Afraid of slipping off. Must be the leather. . . . But, of course, it depends on the gender of the person one's thinking of, if one's thinking of a man or a woman.

TOMAS

So, who are you thinking of?

FRANK

Jenna.

TOMAS

Jenna?

FRANK

Yes, you know. Katarina is leaving for Milan on Tuesday. A trade show, a furniture show.

TOMAS

Really.

FRANK

Yes, Italian furniture is getting really hot, feels new and tough. Sofas and horse blankets.

TOMAS

Are you going too?

FRANK

You think I should? Do you like pornography?

TOMAS

Pornography?

FRANK

Yes. Do you like pornography?

TOMAS

No.

FRANK

But I do.

TOMAS

Why do you ask?

FRANK

I don't know. . . . Don't you like any kind of pornography?

TOMAS

No . . . why?

FRANK

Do you like sex when it's brutal? (*sits down in the chair*) I like any kind of sex . . . as long as it's brutal. (*pause*) Any kind of brutality as long as it's sexual. . . . What would you say if I would bend forward? Well, it might be a little too far, but if I stood up . . . and would go up to you and turn my hand like this and caress your cock through your pants . . . up like this . . . and then down, and back and forth . . . how about it? May I take it out and hold it? . . . No? . . . May I put my cock in your anus? May I push my cock into your anus? Twice? Why can't I put my cock in your anus? Do you never long for that? (*pause*) I like it so much. I think it's beautiful. Don't you like any kind of pornography? (*Tomas doesn't know what to say.*) I do. I think it's so beautiful.

TOMAS

Really.

(*pause*)

FRANK

I think it's beautiful to see two men kissing. I think that's wonderful.

TOMAS

We don't really know each other.

FRANK

You and me? . . . God no, no, no, no . . . I wasn't thinking of you and me but, in general, men in general, who kiss each other on the mouth. (*pause*) We don't know each other. I usually don't talk this frankly. Do you really think I would talk to my colleagues like this, at lunch? . . . My God, that wouldn't work. They are like big kids, big boys, big guys . . . they need a daddy. They need a big daddy with a big cock, one that they can kneel in front of and suck. . . . That's what it's all about . . . haven't you understood that? . . . But they don't dare to admit it, and still they have such problems, such pain . . . they don't want to admit it. . . . That's why they find one woman after another and keep making babies that they can't take care of, and they drink and scream and soil themselves. . . . But do you think they want to talk about it when they sit there in the darkness? They can't. No, instead they continue to hunt for young girls. (*Frank picks up the crystal vase off the table.*) Look at the color of the sky on the other side, it's unreal. . . . Can't you find your glasses?

TOMAS

No.

FRANK

(*calmly throws the heavy, thin crystal vase to Tomas*) That's too bad. . . . (*carefully*) I don't know if I can talk to you about these things. . . . Can I?

TOMAS

(*who has caught the vase, throws it just as calmly back*) What?

FRANK

(*catching the vase*) About the stuff . . . that I'm trying to talk to you about . . . can I?

TOMAS

Well . . . try . . .

(The stage is gradually turning dark. They continue to throw the vase between them, as if the one receiving it can't resist throwing it back.)

FRANK

Yes . . . that's what I'm trying. . . . *(pause)* Didn't you notice?

TOMAS

Maybe . . .

FRANK

What?

TOMAS

Maybe, I said.

FRANK

Maybe?

TOMAS

Well . . . why not?

FRANK

No . . . what did you say?

TOMAS

Right now?

FRANK

Yes.

TOMAS

Nothing. I didn't say anything . . . I'm just looking at you. What?

FRANK

No, nothing . . . nothing at all. . . . I'm sorry.

TOMAS

Sure?

FRANK

Absolutely nothing.

TOMAS

No.

FRANK

No.

TOMAS

What's wrong?

FRANK

My heart.

TOMAS

Your heart?

FRANK

Yes, my heart.

TOMAS

What about it?

FRANK

It's pounding.

TOMAS

Really.

FRANK

Don't you hear it?

TOMAS

No . . . is your heart pounding that hard?

FRANK

Yes, can you hear it . . . do you hear it?

TOMAS

No.

FRANK

I get so nervous.

TOMAS

Why?

FRANK

I don't know.

TOMAS

Yes, you seem really nervous.

FRANK

It happens very easily to me. That's just how it is.

TOMAS

Are you getting tired?

FRANK

Why do you ask?

TOMAS

Just think if I drop it?

FRANK

(*calmly*) No, don't do that. It's valuable.

TOMAS

Don't tell me that.

FRANK

It was my mother's.

TOMAS

How valuable?

FRANK

It's just an ordinary crystal vase.

TOMAS

I'm not going to drop it.

FRANK

No, I didn't think so. That's not what I meant.

                    TOMAS
What did you mean then?

                    FRANK
I just said it.

                    TOMAS
I don't think it'll break if you drop it.

                    FRANK
No. Probably not.

                    TOMAS
No.

                    FRANK
(*stands up, walks in a circle around Tomas*) Shall we change hands?

                    TOMAS
Sure.

                    FRANK
Didn't you ever kiss a man?

                    TOMAS
A man?

                    FRANK
Yes, in an erotic way?

                    TOMAS
On the mouth?

                    FRANK
On the lips?

                    TOMAS
Directly on the mouth?

                    FRANK
With your tongue?

TOMAS

With my tongue?

FRANK

Deep inside?

TOMAS

How?

FRANK

With the tongue deeply, deep inside his mouth?

TOMAS

Why do you ask?

FRANK

Do you understand?

TOMAS

No.

FRANK

While sober, I mean.

TOMAS

Are you thinking of anyone special?

FRANK

Why do you think that?

TOMAS

Why would I have done that?

FRANK

Haven't you ever longed to do it?

TOMAS

Have you?

FRANK

Sober, you mean? . . . I really never drink like this. I get a little weird from it. I never get drunk. Are you drunk now?

TOMAS

Sorry?

FRANK

Tomas . . .

TOMAS

Yes.

FRANK

Do you feel like kissing me right now?

TOMAS

Kiss you?

FRANK

Yes . . . why don't you kiss me right now. Quickly.

TOMAS

(*stands up*) Then I have to put down the vase.

FRANK

Sure, of course, me too.

TOMAS

Why don't you stop throwing it then?

FRANK

Why don't you stop catching it.

TOMAS

That's worse.

FRANK

Yes . . . I understand.

TOMAS

We can stop at the same time.

FRANK

(*pause*) At the same time?

TOMAS

Yes, that's how it has to be. Both of us.

FRANK

(*pause*) How?

TOMAS

If you don't throw it, I won't catch it.

FRANK

 I'd rather not catch it.

TOMAS

Do you think it feels heavier?

FRANK

No, it's getting lighter.

TOMAS

I hope this isn't the urn?

FRANK

No, it's the vase.

TOMAS

It's going slower and slower.

FRANK

I can't stop.

TOMAS

Just think if you throw it the wrong way.

FRANK

How?

TOMAS

(*forces Frank backwards towards the front door*) Just think if I throw it
in your face?

FRANK

That would be terrible.

TOMAS

Are you scared?

FRANK

Yes. Always.

TOMAS

Of what?

FRANK

None of your business.

TOMAS

Accepted.

FRANK

Okay.

TOMAS

I couldn't care less.

FRANK

Well, you're right . . . women most of all, embracing, being in the same bed, eating together, flushing the toilet after them, holding their hands. I can't stand it. . . . Do you like it? When I'm in bed with a woman and she has fallen asleep—they have such incredible talent for sleeping, as if nothing could happen to them—I lay awake by her side and I look at her and I think now, now is the moment for a happy little murder, now I'll kill her. I feel such desire to kill the poor woman, poor little one, who has only me . . . (*He throws the vase into the wall of the bathroom through the open door. It breaks.*) Women always want us to be as bad as they don't want us to be. They manage to succeed in making us look bad. . . . Haven't you ever felt the desire to kill? Never? . . . Are you sure? They just want more and more. (*very upset, serious*) Tomas . . . don't you understand? . . . I feel like I'm drowning. . . . Dear Tomas, Tomas, come here . . . Tomas . . . I want you to kiss me . . . dear Tomas . . . we're the only ones here.

TOMAS

What?

FRANK

It's just us here. Come here and kiss me.

TOMAS

Are you crazy?

FRANK

I'm lonely. I'm so lonely.

TOMAS

Fuck off.

FRANK

I don't even know my name anymore. . . . What's my name?

TOMAS

Don't touch me. . . . I'll kill you.

FRANK

No, don't talk like that. . . . I'm coming over to you.

TOMAS

Then I'll kill you.

FRANK

I'm so lonely. I'm ready to explode but no one notices. (*Katarina comes back, goes to the table, and pulls off the wet, torn dress. She is naked except for her underwear.*) Yes, here we are talking . . . (*pause*) Listen old buddy, shouldn't you go downstairs and get your wife? What do you think she's doing? Crying? Is she the suicidal kind who suddenly leaps out the window or is she just getting fatter and fatter? . . . Darling, aren't you cold? But dear Katarina, do put something on your body. (*pause*) This is my home. I said this is my home. (*to Tomas*) You see, this is the situation. My brother and his wife were supposed to have been sleeping over here tonight. Tomorrow we're going to a funeral. My mother is dead. I'm responsible for her ashes. They are over there. Don't you understand? It . . . can be too much. There are things you simply don't do. (*Frank goes over to Katarina.*) Enough. Let's have no more of this. Am I right? Katarina, it's enough.

KATARINA

No, don't touch me.

FRANK

Think of Mom.

KATARINA

Don't touch me.

FRANK

What are you talking about? I'm not going to touch you.

KATARINA

You better fucking not.

FRANK

I'm just trying to be friendly.

KATARINA

You can stuff your friendliness up your ass. I don't want it.

FRANK

No?

KATARINA

No.

FRANK

Well then. (*to Tomas with a smile*) It seems like we are in the middle of our sixteenth divorce. I hope you don't mind. Have you found what you were looking for? (*pause*) If I were you I'd go downstairs and check if she's okay. . . . I thought there was a strange karma surrounding her. Maybe she's slept too much or too little. I mean it doesn't seem very good her dropping the kid and all that, twice in the same night. Of course it's probably worse to drop grownups, but kids can easily think it's a bad habit. . . . Do you want me to go in your place and find out how every-thing is? Would you mind? (*pause*) I think I'll go downstairs and talk to her. Maybe she needs someone. She might think we don't like her. I think I'll go downstairs.

KATARINA

Yes, you do that.

FRANK

Get her away from her thoughts . . . since no one else will. Since no one else will, I said. (*to Katarina, who is on her way to the kitchen*) You know, I've seen men with bigger boobs. No, indeed, no, we aren't going to have that much fun . . . no, I think I'll have another drink. I might as well get plastered. Right? . . . Since tomorrow is . . . what do I want now? (*Frank goes to the kitchen, picks up the flowers from the floor and gives them to Katarina.*) Here, darling. (*tries to caress her back*) Hope you aren't getting cold. (*Katarina accepts the flowers.*) It wasn't that long ago we stood like this and said "I love you."

KATARINA

That was very long ago.

FRANK

But it feels like it wasn't that long ago. (*Katarina pushes the flowers into Frank's face.*) Now you've tried a door. Try the window. Why don't you throw yourself out like the wife of Modigliani?

KATARINA

She did it out of love.

FRANK

(*to Tomas*) We have no other means of expression. It's terrible. We should leave each other for a while. We should see . . . a family therapist. No, we already did. I don't know what we should do. I should go somewhere. I should really just leave. If I weren't so tired.

KATARINA

Why don't you.

FRANK

Where to? (*pause*) Where?

KATARINA

The emergency room at the psychiatric clinic.

FRANK

No one is waiting for me there either. . . . If there only was someone to go to, anyone.

KATARINA

Bring the urn.

FRANK

What did you say?

KATARINA

Bring the urn.

FRANK

Yes, I will. Do you really think I'd leave it here?

KATARINA

Go down to Jenna. She has boobs enough for two.

FRANK

What did you say? (*to Tomas*) Is she allowed to say such naughty things about your little wife? Doesn't it make you angry?

KATARINA

Tomas knows . . . what I mean.

FRANK

He does?

KATARINA

He understands very well why I said it. (*laughs*) So, go downstairs. Nothing will happen anyway. . . . She thinks you are awful.

FRANK

No, I'm not leaving. I'm staying here. (*pause*) I'm going nowhere. I'm staying here.

KATARINA

Of course you are. Of course you are. Of course you are.

FRANK

Yes. (*pause*) That's right. This is my apartment. I'm the one paying the rent.

KATARINA

Just stand there and pull on your cuffs, you idiot.

TOMAS

What cuffs?

KATARINA

Look at him. (*They look at him. Tomas doesn't understand.*) Look at how he pulls the cuffs down over his hands, just like people who are going . . . insane, who've almost gone insane, further and further down over his hands, until you only see his finger tips. That's when you're sick.

TOMAS

I never thought about that.

FRANK

(*turns on the radio, hears an Italian singer*) But Katarina does. She always thinks about those things.

KATARINA

Please notice. There are loads of small, interesting signs one can learn to recognize. It's interesting.

TOMAS

(*by the kitchen door*) There really is something to that. That's true.

FRANK

I believe you.

TOMAS

Look at you . . . you've pulled your shirt almost all the way down to your knees. (*He takes hold of Frank's cuffs and holds them.*)

FRANK

(*He rips himself loose from Tomas's grip and pushes him so that he falls on the floor with more force than he thought he had and hisses resolutely.*) You little gnat; next time you try something like that, don't forget to bring your hat, so that you'll have something to put your brain in.

TOMAS

(*rushes up, runs towards Frank*) Well, now, you fucking son of a bitch, I've had enough! I'm going to give it to you!

FRANK

You're worse than a bad joke . . . believe me.

TOMAS

(*hits him*) You fucking fag. I'm going to plaster you to the wall.

FRANK

I haven't seen people like you since 1965. I didn't think that people like you were still around.

TOMAS

(*He continues to hit him. Frank falls to the floor.*) Be careful, you fucking fag.

KATARINA

Go ahead, hit him. It doesn't matter to me . . . it's over!

FRANK

Fag?

KATARINA

Stuff him in the refrigerator.

TOMAS

He tried to touch me while you were out. He tried to grope me.

FRANK

You must've misunderstood.

TOMAS

Get up so that I can hit you again.

FRANK

No, I'm fine here.

KATARINA

See, you aren't that tough any more, now that you're fighting a man.

TOMAS

Stand up, I said.

FRANK

Why? Why don't you bend down if you want to hit me? (*Tomas kicks him.*) I'm not competing and I'm not interested in measuring cocks.

TOMAS

(*speaking at the same time*) Do something, then. I don't want to kill him. Tell him to stay where he is.

FRANK

Not on any level, so to speak. There he stands measuring his cock. Measuring and measuring. (*Tomas kicks him again.*)

KATARINA

How does it feel, Frank?

FRANK

I feel nothing.

TOMAS

Aren't you going to defend yourself?

FRANK

I guess you'll get tired soon.

KATARINA

What the hell, Frank, stand up. (*to Tomas*) Leave him; come, let's go.

TOMAS

Where?

KATARINA

(*goes to the hallway*) Wherever, the park. Do you hear what I'm saying?

FRANK

Sure.

KATARINA

I'm leaving now.

FRANK

Sure, you do that.

KATARINA

Now I hope you feel really good. I hope it hurts like crazy, so that you'll know how it has been for me. (*She goes to the kitchen, bends down, and caresses Frank's cheek.*) Do you hear me? Why don't you answer me?

FRANK

What do you want me to say? (*silence*)

KATARINA

I've had enough of you . . . I need love (*Tomas goes to Katarina in the kitchen.*)

FRANK

Stay away from me.

KATARINA

(*She goes out to the hallway. Tomas follows.*) Yes, I will. I'm letting go of you.

FRANK

Be my guest.

KATARINA

Don't think that you'll find any peace and quiet when I'm gone. (*pause*) Do you hear what I'm saying? Don't think you'll just lie down and sleep and get away from everything. (*Katarina goes to the table. Frank stands up in the kitchen and goes into the hallway.*)

FRANK

What do you mean by that?

KATARINA

I hope you'll suffer as much as I have.

FRANK

(*towards Katarina*) I'm not going to suffer. Please leave, so that I'll be able to clean up this mess and relax a little.

KATARINA

You won't be able to relax. You'll die.

FRANK

(*calmly*) Really, why? (*Frank hits Katarina with his arm on her neck. She falls into the chair. Katarina screams. Jenna opens the door.*)

SCENE SEVEN

KATARINA

Because I'm leaving you . . . because that's what I'm doing, Frank. . . .

FRANK

Good, but hurry up then.

KATARINA

But don't you understand? You'll die.

FRANK

No, I won't. I don't want you in my bed. You can't give me anything but a stomach ache. Tonight I'll sleep for ten hours and in the morning I'll straighten up in here. I'm going to have a wonderful time and a clean house.

JENNA

(*She carefully closes the door behind her, excusing herself, while the others look at her. Tomas is still standing in the hallway.*) Well, here I am.

FRANK

Finally . . . there you are. . . . I was just about to go and get you.

JENNA

Tomas.

FRANK

Come in. (*He goes to the kitchen and turns off the radio.*)

JENNA

Dear Tomas . . .

FRANK

(*by the kitchen door*) We were worried. . . . Come in and sit down. I'm allowed to ask, am I not? Are you feeling any better?

JENNA

I haven't been sick.

FRANK

Everything feels much better now. I'll get you something to drink. (*He goes over to the table with all the bottles of booze.*) One would think we were airline hostesses, Katarina and I; no furniture, just expensive booze everywhere. But it is because I don't drink that we have so much booze everywhere. Aren't you coming in?

JENNA

(*still by the door*) Dear Tomas? (*Tomas can't answer.*) Why don't you answer me?

TOMAS

What do you want me to say?

JENNA

(*stares at him*) Tomas . . . (*Tomas goes to the chair.*)

FRANK

(*goes out to the hallway*) Come, come, I'll show you the urn. (*picks up the plastic bag from the shelf*)

JENNA

Dear Tomas . . . I don't want to just stand here. (*Tomas sits down in the chair.*) Why don't you come downstairs with me, right now? Why don't we go down to our home? (*Tomas looks at Katarina.*)

FRANK

(*to Jenna*) He'll be there. Don't worry. There's nothing dangerous here.

JENNA

(*still staring at Tomas*) I don't want anything.

FRANK

No, you don't have to drink. Just sit here and relax.

JENNA

Did I do something wrong?

FRANK

No, no, not at all.

JENNA

What did I do? (*to Tomas*) Dear Tomas, please answer me?

FRANK

(*puts the plastic bag on the floor*) There . . . sit down and relax.

JENNA

I want to sit with Tomas.

TOMAS

Huh?

JENNA

I want to sit with you.

TOMAS

Sure, sit with me.

JENNA

(*tries to sit in the chair*) It won't work. There's no room for me. (*stands up*) I'll sit in your lap?

TOMAS

What the hell is wrong with you? Sit by yourself. (*Jenna tries to sit in his lap. He pushes her away and she falls on the floor. Jenna starts to cry.*)

FRANK

There, there, don't be upset (*Frank goes to the table to get a drink. There is silence.*)

TOMAS

(*to Jenna*) What's wrong with you? Are you crying?

FRANK

No, no.

JENNA

Only tears.

TOMAS

Why the hell are you bawling? What did I do now? Am I not allowed to sit here?

JENNA

Why don't we go home?

TOMAS

I'll go when I want to.

JENNA

It's late . . . I'm not feeling any better.

TOMAS

No, I noticed. You never do.

FRANK

Here you are. (*gives her a glass*)

JENNA

(*takes it*) No, I don't want any more. (*He gives the glass to Tomas, who doesn't accept it.*) Really. I don't want any more. (*Katarina stands up and goes toward the bedroom. Tomas follows her with his eyes.*)

FRANK

Don't mind Katarina . . . forget her for a while, she'll be back soon. (*He laughs. Frank sits in the chair.*) I've seen bigger boobs on men, really, and they were prettier.

JENNA

(*laughs*) Sorry. (*drinks*)

FRANK

No problem.

JENNA

I just came up to get Tomas.

FRANK

I understand. But it doesn't seem like he wants to leave.

JENNA

No, I don't understand why . . . why don't you want to come home with me?

(*All four are silent.*)

FRANK

By the way, I have something for you, before I forget. (*Frank puts his drink down, takes the poster, and gives it to Jenna.*) Please. It's for you.

JENNA

What?

FRANK

Please.

JENNA

Why?

FRANK

Pick it up.

JENNA

But no . . .

FRANK

Yes, I said.

JENNA

(*picks it up and looks at it*) It's really lovely.

FRANK

Since you liked it. . .

JENNA

But I can't accept it.

FRANK

You already did. (*sits down in the chair again*)

JENNA

It's very nice . . . how kind of you. Thank you very much.

FRANK

It's nothing. I'm tired of realistic art.

JENNA

Oh, it's really so nice. (*drinks*)

FRANK

Yes.

JENNA

I don't know where I'm going to put it.

TOMAS

Are you kidding?

JENNA

I think I'll put it in the dining room.

KATARINA

It was given to me, but it doesn't matter.

JENNA

Oh really . . . then I can't take it. I didn't know.

KATARINA

Keep it. I don't want anything that's his. Let him piss on me. (*to Frank*)
It's just to hurt me, that you want to make her happy. It doesn't work.

FRANK

I wasn't thinking of you at all . . .

JENNA

(*nervously*) But I'm not at all happy. . . . Sorry. (*drinks*)

KATARINA

But dear, it doesn't matter.

FRANK

No, no, absolutely not. (*pause*) It's a wonderful night.

JENNA

Yes.

FRANK

The curtains are fluttering, the doves are muttering . . .

JENNA

There's one that's so cute. I think she has little ones in the park.

FRANK

Do you want a caffe latte, Peggy?

TOMAS

Peggy?

FRANK

(*surprised*) Huh?

TOMAS

Huh, that's not her name. Her name isn't Peggy.

FRANK

No? Sorry. I just said that it's a beautiful night.

TOMAS

Don't screw with me. (*pause*) You know what will happen. Don't screw with me.

FRANK

No, then I'd have my hands full. (*pause*)

TOMAS

What do you mean by that?

FRANK

So, you woke up?

TOMAS

You heard me . . . I'm not impressed. Not by anything.

FRANK

(*to Tomas and Jenna*) You're very strange, the two of you.

JENNA

What?! The two of us? (*Katarina is standing by the bedroom door looking very intoxicated.*)

TOMAS

Yes?

(*pause*)

FRANK

Yes . . . but not as strange as Katarina. She's mentally ill. . . . I feel sorry
for her.

TOMAS

(*looks at Katarina*) Now he's starting again. This is unbearable.

JENNA

Why can't we go home?

TOMAS

Why? . . . If you want to go, go!

FRANK

She's crazy. That's all I know. What do we know about people like that?
Look at her. It's all theatre. Just wait, Tomas, soon she'll start to play
"dog without owner" again.

JENNA

He doesn't want to play anything. He has to go downstairs and go to bed
because it's getting late. He's working tomorrow. We aren't used to
being up this late. He's tired. I can see how tired he is.

FRANK

Katarina usually gets what she wants. If she has decided that Tomas is
going to fuck her, I don't think your tits will be enough, Jenna, believe
me. (*Katarina opens the bedroom door.*)

JENNA

What are you saying?

FRANK

You have to keep a sense of reality. Sometimes she does. When it's necessary. Most of the time she does not. I'm the one who has to . . . look at
her. (*Frank stands up and goes towards the bedroom. Katarina runs into
the bedroom and closes the door.*) What are you doing, Katarina? Was I
too mean?

JENNA

What are you saying?

                        FRANK

Doesn't matter. Don't listen to me. That was a terrible thing to say. I'm
terrible.

                        JENNA

Yes, you are.

                        FRANK

I know. (*takes her hand, holds it*) You're a kind person.

                        JENNA

Who . . . me?

                        FRANK

Yes. You are kind.

                        JENNA

No, I'm not.

                        FRANK

Yes, you are. You must be.

                        JENNA

No, I'm not.

                        FRANK

Sure you are. I can feel it.

                        JENNA

That's the worst thing one can say about a person.

                        FRANK

Yes, if that's the only thing one can say. But that's not what I said. I said
"You're kind." . . . Do you understand? I'm trying to express myself as
clearly as possible. . . . You aren't just kind . . . there's something else
about you . . . something extraordinary.

                        JENNA

Really. . .what?

                        FRANK

You cry because you're sad. . . . Do you know what I mean?

JENNA

I'm so uninteresting.

FRANK

No, you've got something . . . something extraordinary . . .

JENNA

What are you talking about?

FRANK

Yes . . . a ray of light . . . something divine . . . a ray of unselfishness.

JENNA

Wow . . . thank you.

FRANK

Don't thank me. Don't thank me for that. Then it won't mean anything.

JENNA

That was beautiful.

FRANK

Did you like it?

JENNA

It was just beautiful.

FRANK

Yes, that's what Tomas said, too.

TOMAS

Are you really having another drink? Haven't you had enough?

JENNA

(*She looks at her glass, which is empty.*) Wow, I didn't realize . . . what did Tomas say?

FRANK

About what, Jenna?

JENNA

About me?

FRANK

Are you feeling better now?

JENNA

A little . . . but I better not drink any more . . . then I'll just start crying.

TOMAS

Yes, and I'm tired of it.

FRANK

You never say anything mean or demeaning about people, because you know it'll come back to you. . . . Am I right?

JENNA

What did Tomas say? What did he say?

FRANK

He said that you aren't aggressive. It's terrible, she's not aggressive, she's always horny.

JENNA

Horny?

FRANK

Yes, instead of being angry.

JENNA

Horny? Me?

FRANK

Yes.

TOMAS

(*He turns his chair towards Jenna and Frank.*) You better watch it. For the last time, I'm telling you . . .

FRANK

So, he wants to fight again. He's strange. He must be feeling threatened.

TOMAS

(*stands up*) I'm warning you.

FRANK

Yes, I hear you.

TOMAS

I mean it. I'll flush you down the toilet. I'll wipe the floors with you. (*Jenna is trying to stop Tomas, who pushes her away.*)

FRANK

Yes, yes, I believe you.

TOMAS

Look, I've been listening to you all night and I'm tired of it. I'm not an idiot.

JENNA

Tomas, let's go home. It's no use. Come on, let's go. (*She forces Tomas to go backwards.*)

TOMAS

(*He pushes Jenna and happens to tear her white glove.*) What the hell, stop it.

JENNA

But Tomas dear, why are you so angry?

TOMAS

Stop nagging me. You aren't a kid any more. . . . If you want to go down and go to bed, why the hell don't you!? Go to bed . . . I'm not running away! You know I always come home! You know I haven't been gone a single night for twelve years since we were married! What do you think might happen? Am I not allowed to look at faces other than yours? What's wrong with you? Why the hell can't I talk about anything but the kids and who they've played with . . . and their fuckin' parents . . . how they look in the mornings and how strange they are? You don't do anything but gossip about others and talk about how great we are! Are we? Are we great? Is everything really great with us!?

JENNA

Yes but, compared to others . . .

TOMAS

You don't know how it is for me . . . you've no idea how it is for me!

JENNA

Dear Tomas, why don't we talk about this another time? I get so frightened when you scream like this.

TOMAS

What the hell . . . why are you so frightened? Go to bed. Go downstairs and wait. I'll be there. I'll be there when I feel like it . . . if I feel like it, then I'll be there.

JENNA

I don't want to leave without you.

TOMAS

Well, just stand there then. (*pause*) I'm tired of you.

JENNA

What . . . what are you saying?

TOMAS

You heard me.

JENNA

Are you angry? . . . What did I do?

TOMAS

I'm tired of you. Don't you hear me?

JENNA

Dear Tomas . . . dear Tomas . . .

TOMAS

I can't stand looking at you. That's how I feel.

JENNA

That's just because you've been drinking.

TOMAS

No, the hell it is! I can't stand looking at you any longer. Do you hear me!? (*He goes up to her and screams in her face.*) I can't stand looking at you any longer. (*Jenna starts to cry. She is standing in front of the broken kitchen door. Tomas is shaking her.*) So now she's crying again.

JENNA

I'm so sad.

TOMAS

Yes, I could live without that. (*Jenna is crying quietly with open eyes.*) You'll have to drool on someone else, I'm going to sit here. (*Tomas sits in the chair.*) Why don't you run down to your little doll house and start painting your kitchen red . . . or whatever the fuck it is that you've planned for us to do for fun this summer!

JENNA

I'm sorry. Give me a kiss.

TOMAS

What?

JENNA

I'm sorry. Kiss me. (*She kisses him.*) More. No, I want a kiss with your mouth open.

TOMAS

Sit down! Aren't you leaving? You stick to me like a tick on my ass.

JENNA

I don't want to go downstairs by myself. (*Jenna sits in the chair, still holding the poster.*) I'll never go downstairs ever again, if you don't want me there. . . . Do you hear me?

TOMAS

Sure, stay . . . sit there and keep watch over me. . . . Let the kids die, what do I care?

JENNA

I'm staying.

TOMAS

Fuck, why are you screaming? . . . Why do you do that? What joy do you get from that?

JENNA

No joy at all.

TOMAS

I don't give a damn about what you do.

JENNA

What's wrong with me?

FRANK

(*goes to the bedroom door*) Where's Katarina?

TOMAS

Why are you so wet? You look like a big fetus. (*Frank laughs at Katarina, who's coming back. She's dressed in a very beautiful, formerly white but, at this point, yellowed dress.*) They're laughing at you. . . . Why?

JENNA

Because I'm funny.

FRANK

Hello, Katarina.

KATARINA

Hello, Frank.

FRANK

How are you?

KATARINA

I feel much better.

FRANK

That makes me happy.

KATARINA

(*She goes towards Tomas.*) I simply have to.

JENNA

What a wonderful dress.

KATARINA

Do you like the color?

JENNA

Yes, well, it's beautiful. . . . White? But look, there's nothing that's green in here, nothing that's green.

KATARINA

(*to Frank, filled with hate*) Modigliani hated green.

FRANK

(*to Tomas*) Listen, you old drunkard, you, are we friends now? Are we? (*Tomas doesn't answer.*) We really don't have anything to fight about, do we? (*to Jenna*) Is he always like this? Takes everything very personally?

KATARINA

He's impotent.

FRANK

Tomas? I don't think so.

KATARINA

Frank . . .

FRANK

Frank?

KATARINA

Frank is impotent.

FRANK

Really. (*pause*) How?

KATARINA

In other words, he can't fuck . . . poor Frank.

FRANK

(to Jenna) You know how it is. I don't care about her any more.

KATARINA

He can't. I've tried to help him. It's nothing to be ashamed of. I'm not ashamed.

FRANK

(*friendly*) No, shut up, Katarina. This is silly.

KATARINA

You are not alone.

FRANK

Unnecessary. Old conversation for new faces.

KATARINA

In other words, he can't fuck without having fantasies.

FRANK

Oh my God.

KATARINA

Real fantasies . . . do you get it? (*pause*) Lucky that he has so much money, and now you'll have a little more from your little mom. Then we can go to Morocco again . . . where there are so many delicious young boys.

FRANK

Katarina, I don't know if you should be going on like this.

KATARINA

What did you say?

FRANK

I don't know if I'll let you continue.

KATARINA

But you know what I mean? It's not enough with fantasies . . . any longer.

FRANK

What a good time we're having. Tomas's ears are fluttering like bats. Please don't make yourself a worse fool than you already have. (*Frank goes toward Katarina.*)

KATARINA

He wants me to go out to restaurants where there's dancing and find guys to bring home to fuck while he watches and pretends he's my big brother. I guess that soon he'll want me to get paid for it, too. I guess soon he won't even go to work. He's a pimp. You're looking at a pimp.

Frank is a pimp. Look at that pimp. You're a pimp. You're an ordinary Swedish pimp.

FRANK

I don't even answer her anymore. What progress. (*pause*) I didn't hear you. I wasn't tuned to that frequency. I just thought I was. I've really tried tuning in. But seriously, I can't.

KATARINA

I'll stay with you forever as long as you provide me with new boys.

FRANK

Sure.

KATARINA

Well-hung boys, that is.

FRANK

(*He goes to the table to get a drink.*) Well-hung guys, as they say.

KATARINA

That's what he likes. That's what feels good. And I tell you, the way he cries the morning after. On his knees, crying, asking me what I felt, do I love them? "You love me, don't you?" . . . "Of course," I say, "you know I do, you're the one I love." . . . "Dear Katarina, we'll never do this again. I've had enough. This was the last time." But it never is. We've been to Thailand. That was fabulous. Have you been to Thailand?

FRANK

Well, you had to say something, I suppose. You're drunk, aren't you? (*to Jenna*) It's not true.

JENNA

Jesus Christ, why are you like this? I've never seen anything like this before.

FRANK

What? What do you mean? What are we?

JENNA

You are the kind of people who create anxiety in others. . . . I don't like it . . . it's horrible. (*upset*) You're just sitting there not saying anything.

TOMAS

What the hell do you want me to say? This has nothing to do with me. (*He stands up and goes out to the hallway.*)

KATARINA

(*follows after Tomas*) During these nine years that I've been with him, I've followed a golden rule that I've found very helpful. And that is, when he hits me, I'm not the one who's hurting—he is.

FRANK

I give up.

KATARINA

But I can't anymore, I can't stand it anymore . . . (*goes toward Jenna, who's sitting in the chair*) I need help. . . . Jenna, I can't take it anymore.

FRANK

It's not true.

KATARINA

(*She sits down with Jenna, starts to cry.*) I'm so scared, I'm so scared, Jenna. Can I stay with you?

TOMAS

Absolutely.

FRANK

Would you please stop this?

KATARINA

I've got to get away from here. . . . Can I come down with you? Can I sleep in your place tonight? Please, don't leave me alone with him, don't leave me. . . . I don't know what he might do.

JENNA

Of course you can. You can sleep in Sarah's room, since she's with her grandma.

KATARINA

Please forgive me, but I have to get away from here.

TOMAS

Of course.

FRANK

You're horrible. It's horrible to listen to you.

KATARINA

No, no, don't let him get close to me.

FRANK

Are you crazy? I'll never touch you ever again.

KATARINA

Tomas . . .

TOMAS

(*He makes Katarina sit in the chair.*) No, you don't have to be scared. He'll never put his hands on you as long as I'm here. (*Frank takes the package out of the plastic bag.*)

KATARINA

Don't leave me . . . don't leave me here. . . . Why don't we go downstairs right away? Take me away from here. . . . If I could only get some sleep.

TOMAS

Of course we can.

(*Frank takes the urn out of the package, goes over to Katarina, and pours the ashes over her.*)

JENNA

(*stands up*) You can't do that. You shouldn't do that. It's not polite.

FRANK

(*calmly*) One day I'll kill her.

KATARINA

You already did. (*pause*)

JENNA

But you can't do something like that . . . that's not allowed.

(*Katarina stands up, finds the vacuum cleaner and is about to start cleaning up.*)

FRANK

(*He falls on his knees, starts to gather the ashes, and puts them in his pockets while talking. The sound from the vacuum cleaner changes into one long single note.*) I didn't mean to. I'm sorry. Why did I do it? How could I do something like this? What's wrong with me? (*pause*) I didn't think it would be that much. She was so small. Suddenly they become so small. I dreamt about her last night. I usually never dream. Never. I usually never remember my dreams. I don't know why. We were sitting in a room, her and me and Katarina. It was at dusk. Outside there was something going on, a war maybe . . . maybe it was the American Civil War. Mom sat across from me, on the other side of a table, holding a big handbag in her lap. She opened the bag in order to get something. But Katarina told her that I was . . . no, that she would take care of me. She promised she would take care of me and make sure that nothing would happen to me. She tried to convince Mom that I was worth loving, that I had the right to be alive and . . . I was talking the whole time, I don't remember about what. . . . You see, Mom had a revolver in her bag, and as soon as I had to stop talking to catch my breath or something . . . her hand started digging deeper into the bag to get hold of the revolver. The revolver was on its way up the whole time, because she was going to shoot me. But I kept talking and talking so that she had to wait and listen, not in order to hear what I was saying, but because finally the moment would come when I couldn't go on anymore, when I would become silent, and then she would be able to shoot me. But then I suddenly got up and ran to the door and was going to lock it behind me. But then it was transformed into soft drapes and there was no handle. After that I don't know what happened. A mirror . . . a lot of fabric . . . beautiful things . . . a woman, probably a democrat . . . tapestries . . . Why am I here? . . . It's so peaceful here . . . this curtain that is with me . . . it really is talking to me . . . it has a hand. It's as tall as I am. It stands there talking to me. It's putting its hand on my shoulder and asks me to speak more quietly. . . . Am I too loud? . . . Am I shaking? Maybe I could carry the ashes in my hair. (*He takes off both his shoes and socks, puts one shoe back on, starts to put the ashes in the other shoe, and throws ashes in the air.*) What makes me feel good is the thought that you shouldn't be doing this. (*He tastes the ashes and licks his fingers.*) I don't understand how everything escapes me. It all seems so real and substantial, and then, suddenly, it becomes fleeting and it evaporates, like perfume. I used to hate Dag Hammarskjold. I hated him and his tone of voice, mostly his tone of voice. . . . Just once I'd wanted to be heard, and I wanted to touch . . . I'd love to spend time with them again, would like them to . . . that they would come here to me. . . . I'm freezing. Do you know what just happened? The curtain leaned towards me. It's standing here touching my shoulder. . . . What do you want with me? What do you want with me? . . . People are coming out of the kitchen, and there's no one here, and they are not talking. . . . This is difficult. . . . There was one person walking through the room even though there was no one here. . . . This is difficult . . . now it's getting hard. . . . We don't exist. It's horrible. We don't exist. . . . Mom, where are you? Mom? You don't exist. Where are you when you don't exist? Who was my mom? This is hard. This is difficult. I'm crying. (*no tears*) Now something is happening. . . . The curtain is sitting in my lap. . . . What do you want? (*pause*) I'm whispering your name over and over not to go insane. Now, now something very interesting is happening. I stand up. I start to walk. I walk away from here. I leave this room and the people who don't exist. I say goodbye. I walk away. Now I'm leaving. Only the one who leaves will ever return.

(*No one moves. He leaves the room, goes through the front door without closing it behind him, and walks down the stairs. Suddenly Jenna runs after him. She throws the poster on the floor. The sound is again transformed into the sound of the vacuum cleaner. Katarina and Tomas are left standing looking at each other for a long time. Tomas waits. Then he goes towards her and touches her crotch in a brutal manner. The vacuum cleaner is in the way.*)

KATARINA

Ouch! Not so hard. (*sneezes*)

TOMAS

(*He holds on to her in a violent way. She has to bend forward.*) Just think if they come back. Think if they come back.

KATARINA

What about it? Ouch! You're hurting me!

TOMAS

Just think if they come back right now.

KATARINA

Who? Jenna and Frank?

TOMAS

Yes, who else?

KATARINA

You're hurting me.

TOMAS

Oooooh, I can feel it. It hurts like hell. . . . Ouch, ouch, ouch. Doesn't it feel good?

KATARINA

Take it easy. (*sneezes*) (*Tomas is trying to get the vacuum cleaner out of the way. Her bridal veil has been sucked into it.*) My God, such brutality.

TOMAS

Yes. I've been longing for this all night long. I've been sitting here looking at you. I knew I'd have you.

KATARINA

Really . . .

TOMAS

Yes, oh yes.

KATARINA

Come and sit here . . . let's sit down. I don't want to be standing up. (*sits in the chair*)

TOMAS

Watch out not to step on the ashes. God, I can't wait.

KATARINA

I'd rather lie down on the couch.

TOMAS

I can't hear you. I'm just falling . . . kaplonk. (*Tomas lies down on top of Katarina.*)

KATARINA

No . . . no.

TOMAS

Help me get up then. (*Tomas gets up a little.*) Let them have a little fun, but I know they won't.

KATARINA

Not Frank, anyway.

TOMAS

Ha, ha . . . no, not Jenna either! I promise you that!

KATARINA

No? (*pause*)

TOMAS

No, never.

KATARINA

Hasn't she ever been with someone else? . . . Never with someone else?

TOMAS

Are you crazy? (*His hands are deeply in his pockets.*) I don't understand where I put them? I need them. I want to look at you.

KATARINA

Poor Jenna.

TOMAS

Why do you say things like that? . . . She doesn't want to. She likes everything planned in the minutest detail, same thing night after night, and then she thinks we're cutting loose by sitting in the car driving to the country. If we have guests she goes out of her mind, as if it was the hardest thing in the world. You have no idea how many times I've bumped into you in the hallway, when I've been thinking . . . because you're walking so fucking slowly up the stairs, and you breathe as if you'd been running several miles . . . that I've been thinking, I'll stick my hand under your skirt and give you a squeeze. . . .

KATARINA

Why didn't you?

TOMAS

Well, I swear you would've been there with your legs apart. Right? Am I right?

KATARINA

Absolutely not.

TOMAS

Let's continue.

KATARINA

How far were we?

TOMAS

Nowhere yet. Let's turn on the light.

KATARINA

Be careful with me. (*sneezes, long pause*)

TOMAS

Do you care at all about me? You don't have to answer. Do you? (*Katarina smiles*.) Don't laugh. (*tenderly*) You don't have to say anything.

KATARINA

No, that's good.

TOMAS

But do you care about me? Can you . . . (*beats his chest*) can you . . . do you understand? . . . Do you see me? Do you know who I am? (*gives up*) No, it doesn't matter . . . it doesn't matter. . . . I can't explain. . . . Do you see what I look like? . . . I? Me?

KATARINA

Sure, the whole time.

TOMAS

How? . . . Do you see me? . . . So answer me then? (*pause*)

KATARINA

Don't talk.

TOMAS

I want to talk! . . . First I want to talk. . . . First I have to talk. . . . I have to talk before . . .

KATARINA

Why?

TOMAS

I don't know. I have to. . . . What are you doing? She's crazy. . . . She . . . she . . . I mean she's yacking and yacking the whole time. . . . It gets on my nerves. I can't talk to her about anything but the kids. We never have a moment to ourselves. Just think if we could leave them somewhere for just one night and drive down to the beach . . . sleep in the car and have some fun. She has never really, really touched me, she . . . or felt the need, I mean. . . . And I've been going to school the whole time, to get away from the lousy jobs I could have in order to get a better lousy job. What a good thing it would be if we could run away from the whole mess, the job, the school loans, the bills.

KATARINA

Even Sarah?

TOMAS

Yes, even Sarah. . . . Every night when I go to bed, I know that that particular day had not been worth anything. Nothing. I'll never remember it. . . . But tomorrow or the week after something will happen, like when we go on vacation . . . when we're stuck in customs in Helsingborg. (*short pause*) Your nipples are incredibly sensitive. . . . You just have to look at them and they stiffen up.

KATARINA

It depends on who's looking at them.

TOMAS

Let's sit somewhere else instead?

KATARINA

You think so? . . . Where?

TOMAS

On the floor.

KATARINA

Sure, that's fine. (*They move down on the floor.*)

TOMAS

Then we'll hear if they come back.

KATARINA

Now what? . . . What are you going to do?

TOMAS

I can't see your face.

KATARINA

Be happy for that. . . . (K*atarina is lying on top of the poster, which wrinkles up.*)

TOMAS

I am. (*He takes off his jacket, rolls it up, and puts it under Katarina's head. Something falls to the floor.*) There's ashes on the jacket, too.

KATARINA

Now I'm comfortable . . . I'm longing for you.

TOMAS

Me?

KATARINA

Yes.

TOMAS

You are?

KATARINA

Now, now, I'm longing for you . . . my paws are warm. (*pause*) I say such dumb things. (*pause*)

TOMAS

Well . . . I like it.

KATARINA

How's this?

TOMAS

Good. . . . What do you think they're doing?

KATARINA

Nothing. Not Frank. He only cares about me.

TOMAS

They are probably sitting by Wolfgang's crib. I wonder if he might get some dumb idea of throwing him up in the air. (*looks up toward the ceiling*) That wouldn't be good. He's too little for that.

KATARINA

But I never . . . I haven't promised him anything. I did tell him that our relationship never had time to get started. Then he began to cry. He started to cry.

TOMAS

Really . . .

KATARINA

In the coffee shop above the gym.

TOMAS

Really, in the coffee shop.

KATARINA

He says such terrible things. He's so dramatic. I love it.

TOMAS

(*thinks someone is coming*) Be quiet.

KATARINA

What?

TOMAS

Be quiet.

KATARINA

It's nothing dangerous.

TOMAS

I don't feel so good.

KATARINA

(*to herself*) But you're the one I've been waiting for my whole life.

TOMAS

Me?

KATARINA

Or someone like you.

TOMAS

Like me . . . how?

KATARINA

I want to do so many things with you.

TOMAS

I really don't feel so good.

KATARINA

We'll travel a lot.

TOMAS

I usually don't drink this much.

KATARINA

I'd really like to go away with you. Do you like getting a blow job? Do you like that? (*sneezes*)

TOMAS

Listen, I've got to stand up for a little while. I feel such pressure in my stomach.

KATARINA

Have you ever had that done to you?

TOMAS

Just move over a little . . .

KATARINA

Why don't we go to the bedroom?

TOMAS

You don't think he'd start hitting her or something like that? (*pause*)

KATARINA

Come, come with me. (*Katarina pulls Tomas into the bedroom.*) Can't you at least lie on top of me?

TOMAS

Now? (*He absentmindedly pulls her dress high up over her thigh, and she lifts herself toward him. He caresses her thigh and touches her dress.*) What a strange dress.

KATARINA

You think so?

TOMAS

What's it made of?

KATARINA

Happiness.

TOMAS

Where did you find it?

KATARINA

(*lies down on the bed*) It's my wedding dress. Come and lie down on top of me for a little while. (*Tomas lies down on top of her; she grunts. They are on top of the hairdryer, which starts up.*)

TOMAS

Hey, you.

KATARINA

(*turns off the hairdryer*) No, don't say anything.

TOMAS

But Katarina.

KATARINA

Be quiet.

TOMAS

I don't feel so good.

KATARINA

Oh dear, dear . . . you haven't even kissed me.

TOMAS

No, not now.

KATARINA

Yes, yes.

TOMAS

Katarina . . . I don't feel so good.

KATARINA

No, don't talk.

TOMAS

But Katarina, listen, listen to me . . . it's true.

KATARINA

You don't have to talk. . . . You don't have to say anything. It's better if you don't talk. Kiss me instead!

TOMAS

Wait.

KATARINA

I need it. I need to feel you, just for a little while. Otherwise I'll go crazy. (*She pulls his head down and gets him to kiss her. Tomas suddenly feels very sick after his alcohol consumption, gets up, and runs into the living room. Katarina remains on the bed.*)

TOMAS

(*comes back, stops in the doorway*) Sorry . . . where are you?

KATARINA

Here.

TOMAS

Sorry.

KATARINA

It doesn't matter.

TOMAS

But I really want to . . . sorry . . . I've been dreaming of this for years.

KATARINA

What?

TOMAS

Of you . . . I told you that.

KATARINA

You did?

TOMAS

And now that I finally have a chance to fuck you, this happens.

KATARINA

Just take it easy. . . . Of course you'll fuck me.

TOMAS

I feel sick.

KATARINA

Inside me. You'll like it. . . . It will be difficult for me. (*Katarina on her knees in front of Tomas*) What do you say? What do you want me to do?

TOMAS

Nothing . . . I don't feel very well . . . I feel sick . . . and I don't want to hurt her . . . it's unnecessary. (*Katarina starts to laugh and pulls Tomas down.*) Yes, you can say whatever you want. I just don't want to! I don't feel like it . . . that's all I have to say . . . I don't feel like it anymore. I'm really sorry. It's not your fault. (*He pulls away. Katarina is still on the floor, laughing.*) Yes, that's how it is. I can't do anything about it. It's nothing to laugh at. . . . What the hell, stop laughing!

KATARINA

I've stopped.

TOMAS

It's nothing to laugh at. I'd do it if I could. . . . It happens by itself. I can't do it just because you want it. You understand that, don't you? . . . I don't know you. . . . (*Katarina is sitting on the bed.*) You probably still like him a lot . . . you probably really like him, I said.

KATARINA

Who?

TOMAS

Ka ka ka . . . What the hell is his name?

KATARINA

Frank?

TOMAS

Yes. (*He is starting to shiver, is very cold, his whole body is shaking.*)

KATARINA

Do you mean Frank?

TOMAS

Yes, yes, yes, yes, yes . . .

KATARINA

I love him.

TOMAS

Fffffrank . . . do you mean Fffffrank? Fffffrank, I mean.

KATARINA

I love him.

TOMAS

I'm freezing, I'm shaking, my whole body is shaking. Look . . . brrr. Yes, exactly . . . that's what I'm saying. . . . It's not your fault. . . . Brrr . . . as if I was drunk . . . brrr . . . but if you're going to drink you should really do it. If you're going to drink, you should shut yourself up in an apartment with a woman and lock the door and drink. Then you can do anything—lick her ass and everything and have fun. (*pause*) Sometimes you have to do some filthy things. . . . Now and then you really have to do some nasty things to feel like a human being.

KATARINA

I love him.

TOMAS

I know. . . . Oh, I'm so cold . . . I'm freezing to death. . . . I don't know why I'm so cold. Are you cold, too? I can't even stand still. . . . Look, I'm jumping up and down. I'm leaving you now.

KATARINA

Yes, why don't you.

TOMAS

I'm going downstairs. . . .

KATARINA

Yes.

TOMAS

I just came up to say hello. I have to leave now. (*starts to shake again*) Now I'm starting again. Brrrrr! Yes, I have to . . . I have to see what she's doing. . . . I have to get there before anything happens. Brrr, it feels good to be this cold, like after a swim in a cold lake. What are you going to do now?

KATARINA

Nothing.

TOMAS

So I'm leaving, then. Just stayed to say goodnight. Will you be all right? Bye, bye.

KATARINA

Bye.

(*Tomas leaves. Katarina is still on the bed. Frank comes in, then Jenna, who closes the door behind them. Frank closes the blinds, goes to the table and steps over things that had fallen down. The room looks terrible.*)

JENNA

I won't leave you. (*She walks behind him the whole time and follows him to the kitchen.*)

FRANK

Why not?

JENNA

I don't know . . . I feel like it's the right thing to do . . . to walk right behind you. . . . (*They go out in the hallway.*)

FRANK

(*brings the radio*) Now I'd like to run to a really difficult place in order to make sure you really are with me, and that you won't give up on me.

JENNA

I won't give up on you. Why don't you sit down? Then I'll sit next to you. (*Frank puts the radio on the floor and sits down on top of the radio. Jenna crouches next to him.*)

FRANK

You're kidding.

JENNA

No.

FRANK

Sure?

JENNA

Please, Frank . . . be serious.

FRANK

(*On his knees by the urn, he puts the radio away and shakes ashes from his hair back into the urn.*) Me, serious?

JENNA

I'd like . . . may I?

FRANK

(*pause*) What kind of kid were you?

JENNA

As a child?

FRANK

Yes.

JENNA

As a little girl? (*pause*)

FRANK

Lonely?

JENNA

Oh no, no, not at all. I was beloved. . . . A small, quiet girl . . . kind, wise, managed very well by myself. (*She sits down on the floor next to Frank.*)

FRANK

Tell me something from your childhood . . . anything.

JENNA

(*thinks for a long time*) I really wanted to go to Sunday school, even though my parents weren't religious . . . because I had heard they gave you a gold star every time you were there, a star that you were supposed to put in your book. And I thought that if I got a star everything would be different. . . . I don't know how, but the first time I went to Sunday school, the teacher told us about Jesus . . . Jesus walking on the water, and I said, "How did he have the guts to do that?"

FRANK

Did you get any stars?

JENNA

Yes, a whole book full of stars. That's all I wanted. . . . May I . . .

FRANK

Did anyone ever say "I love you. I can't live without you?"

JENNA

No.

FRANK

I've got to leave you again. I have to pee.

JENNA

(*stands up*) Then I want to come with you.

FRANK

You may. You make me so happy.

JENNA

Don't talk. When I embrace you it's as if I'd come home. What are you doing?

FRANK

I'm just smiling. You may hold my cock when I pee. Do you want to?

JENNA

Yes. (*They go into the bathroom. Frank pees. They go to the washbasin. He removes the omelet pan from the bowl and Frank helps Jenna wash her hands.*)

FRANK

(*comes out of the bathroom*) Why are you following me everywhere?

JENNA

I don't know. (*He notices small tea candles in the closet.*)

FRANK

Try to explain.

JENNA

No . . . I just feel like it. (*She places a lit candle where he has walked.*)

FRANK

Dear Jenna . . .

JENNA

I can't. I don't have the words.

FRANK

No. Who needs words? (*He goes back to the living room. Jenna continues to light candles.*)

JENNA

Would you have words for this? . . . If it was you?

FRANK

No, that's right . . . you're so different.

JENNA

Why? How?

FRANK

I don't know.

JENNA

No . . . in what way am I different?

FRANK

I don't know, I said.

JENNA

When did it happen? When did you think I was different?

FRANK

(*smiles*) When we kissed. Then you became different. Do you want something?

JENNA

Nothing.

FRANK

Me neither. Do you want to . . . lie down?

JENNA

Yes . . . I can't sleep. (*pause*) That's what Sarah says. She lies there with open eyes and says "I can't sleep. I can't close my eyes. Mommy, I'm not sleeping." And then she's asleep. . . . We had chicken and rice.

FRANK

So you aren't hungry?

JENNA

I don't like eating chicken. When the skin gets in your mouth. Suddenly, derma in your mouth.

FRANK

I'm just going to change clothes, to undress. (*He puts Tomas's glasses on the table next to the telephone, goes to the closet, takes off his shirt, and finds a very old and worn T-shirt.*)

JENNA

I want to take my clothes off, too.

FRANK

Yes.

JENNA

(*She takes off her sweater.*) Is there a shirt I could borrow? (*Frank gives her a T-shirt. He finds a little sailboat in the closet and gives it to Jenna.*)

FRANK

A little gift from me.

JENNA

Thank you.

FRANK

I'm giving it to you for real.

JENNA

It's lovely.

FRANK

I'm just going to the kitchen.

JENNA

Then I'll come too.

FRANK

(*He goes to the kitchen, opens the refrigerator, and pours a glass of milk. Jenna is still placing candles wherever Frank has been.*) Do you want something?

JENNA

No, thanks.

FRANK

Not even frozen Italian . . . Gucci shoes? (*He has taken the shoebox out of the refrigerator and goes back to the living room. Tomas's voice is heard in the telephone: "Jenna! Jenna! Jenna!" Jenna picks up the receiver, still holding Frank's hand.*)

JENNA

Are you taking a shower in the middle of the night? (*puts down the receiver*) It's already daylight outside. Dawn is knocking on the window pane.

FRANK

You don't have to say things like that. (*They sit down, Frank on the chair, Jenna in the armchair, and look at each other. He's drinking milk.*)

JENNA

You've changed.

FRANK

I've changed?

JENNA

Yes . . . very much. (*pause*)

FRANK

Do you want some?

JENNA

No, thanks.

FRANK

Do you know any songs?

JENNA

To sing?

FRANK

Do you know any song to sing, for me, right now, at dawn, when we sit here looking at each other? Do you?

JENNA

Just one.

FRANK

That's enough. Do you like it?

JENNA

Yes, very much.

FRANK

Why don't you sing it, then?

JENNA

For you?

FRANK

Yes . . . just for me. (*pause*) But then I have to hold your hand. I have to hold your hand.

JENNA

So come closer then. (*She pushes the armchair closer to him.*)

FRANK

No, this isn't good . . . we'll lie down. (*Jenna puts the sailboat on the table. Frank lies down next to her. He has pushed the two chairs together.*) Do you have enough room? It feels as if we were three . . . Mom, I mean.

JENNA

What was she like?

FRANK

I remember everybody else, but not her, nothing. . . . Right now I just want you to sing. Wait . . . last night I dreamt about her.

JENNA

Yes, that's what you were telling us.

FRANK

I did? When? I don't remember that. . . . Last night I dreamt I was in the bathroom holding a little plucked chicken in my hands, cold and hard as if it had just been defrosted. I stood holding it over the toilet bowl, and suddenly blood started to come out of its ass. . . . I know it was Mother, and Katarina too, and I heard myself say, "It's an ulcer, it's an ulcer . . ." but it grew in my hands, got bigger and bigger and finally it was so big I couldn't hold it any longer. Why don't you sing now? . . . Now I just want you to sing.

JENNA

(*She is singing, in the beginning carefully and slowly, then with a warm, dark, incredibly beautiful voice.*) I've got no kick from champagne . . .

FRANK

How beautiful.

JENNA

I can't sing. I feel so bashful. I always wanted to be a singer standing on a stage in front of an orchestra.

FRANK

I think you are wonderful. . . . I fell in love with you. (*Tomas's voice in the telephone is saying, "Jenna! Jenna! Jenna!"*) What are you going to do with Tomas? (*Jenna squeezes his hand.*)

JENNA

I don't know, you shouldn't ever try to hold on to someone. It's like sitting on the beach by the ocean playing with the sand. (*reaches out with her hand*) Like this. Look, if you squeeze your hand the sand runs out. If you keep it open, it stays. Now it's your turn to sing for me.

FRANK

No, I don't dare . . . I don't dare . . . I can't.

JENNA

Yes, you do dare.

FRANK

I do?

JENNA

Yes, you have to.

FRANK

(*after a long silence*) You mustn't laugh at me. The whole thing could go to hell . . . but then you have to hold me and not say anything.

(*Katarina is slowly, slowly getting out of bed.*)

JENNA

(*holding his hand*) Oh, your hand . . . your hand.

FRANK

(*He feels something wet on his hand and looks down.*) What was that?

JENNA

Only tears.

FRANK

Are you crying?

JENNA

Tears of love.

FRANK

(*happy*) Are you crying?

JENNA

I'm so happy . . . let me cry. (*She cries quietly while holding his hand, caressing it slowly. Katarina walks slowly towards the door.*)

FRANK

(*touches the tears on her hand*) My beloved.

JENNA

My beloved . . .

FRANK

Do you want to get married now? Or in the spring? (*Jenna is thinking.*)

JENNA

The spring is good, too. (*Jenna turns on the radio, which is on the floor.*)

(*Katarina comes in and walks directly to the closet, holding the hammer and the nails. Frank looks at her, then stands up, and goes up to her as if to take it away from her. She puts her hand lightly on his shoulder.*)

FRANK

What are you going to do? What's going on, Katarina?

(*Everything from now to the end of the play will go extremely slowly, slower than slow. The music changes to one long note. Jenna is in her chair.*)

KATARINA

(*She puts two nails on the table, seems perfectly normal, and forces Frank to walk backwards.*) Don't leave me.

FRANK

When?

KATARINA

Don't leave me.

FRANK

Why not?

KATARINA

Because I love you. Because I love you. You love me.

FRANK

No.

KATARINA

Yes.

FRANK

It's over . . . something . . . has happened.

KATARINA

What?

FRANK

You don't exist for me anymore.

KATARINA

Couldn't you love me anyway?

FRANK

I probably could . . . but I don't want to.

KATARINA

It can't be true.

FRANK

It is.

KATARINA

It's not true. . . . You and I we're so good together. . . . We belong together, and we only need to touch each other to feel it. You only had to smile, and I fell for you. . . . You only had to come through the door and

I was happy again. Yes, we, who suited each other so well, my darling. (*is hugging him*) I really love your face. If you could only be still for three seconds, I'd be there with you for many years. . . . No, spend all my free time there. . . . I love you . . . love you . . . in every kind of way . . . in the deepest part of me I'm ready . . . here and now and always. I know I'll never be able to express it, and that you'll never understand it. I've never really confessed about my disappointment . . . all the small horrors that happen . . . but does it really matter? (*looks up at him*) You only have to be close to me, like last night, and I can live on that for weeks. (*long pause*) My inner self goes between chaos and a great calm. (*pause*) I can still feel the taste of the man you once were . . . still longing for the taste you instilled in me. . . . I'm in love with you again . . . no, infatuated . . . a warm, sincere and loving feeling. . . . I already know we'll have a good life together . . . but I don't dare to repeat what you say when you sit in our bed . . . that we'll take time off, that we'll go away, that we'll be together this summer . . . that you aren't going to work. . . . Today, I think I almost . . . I had the idea that maybe I had to find passion with someone else but you . . . someone who doesn't know who I am, who hasn't seen me, someone I'll probably never meet again. . . . All this just to get where one feels passion, passion. . . . Maybe this is my way of going there all alone. . . . The heart, you say, the heart . . . when I said . . . you're making too much out of love again suddenly. . . you said that you were happy yesterday . . . do you remember? It shows very clearly that you're happy. (*pause*) Suddenly it hits me . . . my paranoia. Is he . . . you . . . happy because he thinks I'm going to leave him . . . and in that way all our problems would be solved? . . . He won't have to feel any guilt towards me . . . that he really doesn't want to be together anymore? Horrible thought . . . still one more horrible thought. . . . Do you know what you want, Frank? Do you know for sure that you want to live with me? . . . Or do you say those things about growing old together just because it sounds charming? (*caresses his face as if she was blind*) Or do you really mean it? . . . I've come to understand a lot tonight. I've come to understand that I love you very much, how much I love you. I hadn't made it clear to myself before, but I've known it. . . . Did I have something in my hand?

FRANK

When you came in here?

KATARINA

Yes, did I carry something?

FRANK

Two nails.

KATARINA

Nothing else?

FRANK

No . . . did you?

KATARINA

A hammer?

FRANK

No, it's over there.

KATARINA

I see. (*She has forced Frank up against the fourth wall, which faces the audience.*) Well, Frank . . .

FRANK

(*smiles*) Well, Katarina . . .

KATARINA

Just think if I took this nail and scratched your hand a little. Think if I scratched you. . . . Just think if I pushed it in harder, so that it would hurt. Just think if I took the hammer and held it up with my hand . . . but, think if I would lift your hand and put it up against the wall like this. I love your hands. (*She performs everything she is talking about, tries it then changes her mind, and finds the best way, without breaking out of her spell. He lets it happen.*) If I would put the nail against your hand and hit this way with the hammer, so that the nail would go right through your hand and deep inside the wall . . . and the same thing with the other hand . . . (*She nails his hands to the wall.*)

FRANK

What are you thinking about?

KATARINA

Nothing.

FRANK

Nothing?

KATARINA

No.

FRANK

Do you love me?

KATARINA

More than ever. It has never changed. I've never loved you less. Only more.

FRANK

Do you still love me?

KATARINA

I've never changed. I've never loved you less. Only more.

FRANK

There isn't much future in that.

KATARINA

That's all the future I need. . . . Do you love me?

FRANK

Yes.

KATARINA

Say it.

FRANK

I love you.

KATARINA

Once more.

FRANK

I love you.

KATARINA

Is it true?

FRANK

Yes.

KATARINA

Say it so that I believe you. Say it so that it works for me.

FRANK

(*He says it in all kinds of different ways.*) I love you. I love you. I love you. I love you. I love you. I love you.

KATARINA

(*as if she was on her death bed*) Don't leave me. . . . I love you so much.

FRANK

What is it that you're doing?

KATARINA

(*She makes a very strong gesture of a sexual nature.*) I'll be your woman all your life. Caress me . . . touch me . . . you have to caress me. . . . I love you. I love you. (*The words become terrifying. She caresses and kisses him all over his body without getting any answer.*) That's the only gift I want. . . . I can only accept that gift. (*The single note changes again to music. The two hundred candles go out at the same time.*)

JENNA

I'm sorry, but you and Frank will have to try to solve your problems yourselves.

(*The white dove flies in through the open window, right into the smoke from the candles. Darkness. After a moment we see the little sailboat in flames, going up in smoke.*)

THE END

ACT

Characters

M, in her late thirties

G, in his early forties

The setting is an examination room in a doctor's office.

Darkness.

Light.

A man and a woman in a room.

A long silence.

                                    G
Good. (*pause*) How are you?

                                    M
Who are you?

                                    G
Yes, that's right. Who am I? (*short pause*) I was just about to introduce
myself. My name is Gott, Mikael Gott. I am a physician.

                                    M
So you think I'm sick.

                                    G
No . . . are you sick?

                                    M
What do you want?

                                    G
Well . . . weren't you informed about that? (*short pause*) That's strange.
Apparently there's been a glitch somewhere. I'm so sorry. I'll have to
talk to them.

                                    M
Who are you?

                                    G
Well . . . as I already told you, I'm a physician. A doctor of medicine. I
graduated from the Medical Academy at Dusseldorf University.

                                    M
Answer my question.

G

Your question? (*short pause*) What question?

M

I asked you who you are. (*pause*) Who are you?

G

I am a physician. A medical doctor. A doctor of medicine. (*smiles*) I think I told you that twice already. In my capacity as a physician I've been asked to meet with you and conduct a medical evaluation of your current medical status. Find out about your general health and such things. (*short pause*) That's why I'm here.

M

Do you believe in God?

G

Do you have any objections?

M

Against God as such, or that you believe in him?

G

Objections regarding me conducting such an evaluation and an update of your medical status.

M

Is that what it's called?

G

I'm sorry?

M

Is that what you call it?

G

Yes, I suppose I do. (*short pause*) What do you mean?

M

An update. Isn't that what you said?

G

Yes, exactly. (*short pause*) I mean, after all, you've lived under rather exceptional circumstances for . . . well, let's see now, how long has it been? How many years have you been here? Is it six or seven years? Six, seven years . . . that is, after all, a rather substantial amount of time under such exceptional circumstances. (*short pause*) What else would this be . . . if not a normal, simple medical checkup . . . that I was asked to perform to the best of my ability?

M

Why not torture?

G

Torture?

M

How old are you?

G

What do you mean? How could it possibly be torture?

M

How old are you?

G

I just want to check your blood pressure, your pulse, heartbeat, EKG, lungs, eyesight, hearing and so on . . . also possibly the pressure in your eyes to see if there are any signs of glaucoma. This is a completely normal health checkup, as far as I understand. Nothing out of the ordinary. Nothing.

M

How old are you? Did your mom buy those glasses for you?

G

My age is irrelevant here. (*short pause*) I'm thirty-six years old. (*short pause*) Why don't we begin?

M

You're the only one who can begin.

(*pause*)

G

Are you bothered by the handcuffs?

M

No. (*short pause*) Are you?

G

I don't know . . . I suppose they are necessary, but somehow it seems inappropriate, I think.

M

You'll get used to them. Where do you live?

G

Excuse me? (*short pause*) Where I live? (*short pause*) I live in Gux-hagen. Not in Cuxhagen but in Guxhagen. It's a suburb of Kassel. Are you familiar with it?

M

Do you really believe that you can get me to think of you as a sympathetic person? Do you for a moment think that you would make me forget who you are? Do you believe that you in some way can make me forget who I am?

G

I think that . . . I think we'll begin the examination. Wouldn't that be good?

M

For whom?

G

What did you say?

M

You said it would be good. I asked, for whom?

G

As far as I can understand it, for both of us. The sooner we're done the better.

M

Have you ever been there?

G
Where?

M
There? Were you ever there?

G
Where have I been?

M
Auschwitz.

G
Auschwitz?

M
Were you ever there?

G
Yes, well . . . I think that . . . I think we'll get going. Do what I came here
to do, the examination. . . . What do you think of beginning with your
eyesight? Just look at the chart hanging over there. Please try to read the
letters on the next to last row while at the same time covering your left
eye with your left hand.

M
Did you go there? Or didn't you go there?

G
Yes. (*short pause*) Of course I've been there. I was there as a visitor. On
a field trip.

M
As a visitor? Are you sure?

G
Yes, I think about ten years ago. . . . Please try to read the next to last
row of letters on the chart hanging over there while you cover your left
eye with your left hand. It won't take long.

M
What did you think?

G

About what?

M

Auschwitz. Was it nice? Pleasant?

G

Auschwitz?

M

Yes, did you find it nice and clean . . . all in all, rather well cared for . . . considering the circumstances?

G

I don't think I would describe it as nice and clean.

M

How, then, would you describe it?

G

Well, as a . . . I'd like to say as a historical place of remembrance, that puts the visitor in a . . . a place that brings the visitor to a moment of grace and stillness while viewing the reality of the past.

M

It couldn't have been easy.

G

On the other hand, who goes there thinking it's going to be easy? But I've heard it so often. I don't feel any guilt. It's not important any more.

M

(*very slowly*) A F I G K H C D O . . .

G

You read the last line. I asked you to read the row of letters above it. (*pause*) Okay, let's proceed with the right eye. Please put your right hand in front of your right eye and read the row of letters above the last line.

M

What time is it?

G

(*looks at his watch*) It seems to be eleven minutes past nine o'clock. You've already been here for eleven minutes.

M

In the morning?

G

In the morning? (*short pause*) No, not at all. It's eleven minutes past nine in the evening. Did you think that right now it's morning? It's not morning. It's evening. Only during evening hours do I have the possibility of accepting work of this nature. In the daytime I have a rather busy medical practice that takes up all my time. Did you really think that right now it's morning? It's not morning, it's evening. (*short pause*) I saw in your medical records that you haven't eaten anything these last five days. Is that correct?

M

Is that what it says?

G

Well?

M

Do you think I'm beautiful?

G

Why? Why aren't you eating?

M

Is that why you're here? Are they afraid I'm going to die?

G

Who?

M

The ones who would like me to die.

G

I don't know who's afraid of what.

M

Do they want me to die?

G

Do you? (*short pause*) Do you want to die?

M

I loved Paris. There I was happy. I think it's the city I like the most, of all the cities I've been to. It's so beautiful. We were free. We were young. Nothing was too late. I could stay up for many nights on end . . . talk to strangers, listen to music, laugh, make love. I never got tired. I loved the scents, the light, the voices, the soft words, the fierce, intense discussions. I used to get an infection in my throat every time I gave my boyfriend a blowjob. I don't remember his name. Is that normal?

G

I don't think that's normal.

M

That I don't remember the name of my boyfriend?

G

Weren't you talking of an infection?

M

No, I was talking about my boyfriend . . . Henrich? . . . I don't remember his name.

G

It's a rather painful and slow way of dying. To starve oneself to death, I mean. I mean, it takes a rather long time.

M

Three months?

G

More like two, I think.

M

Just two? Is it that fast? That's doable, I guess.

G

It depends on your general health. Is that what you're planning to do?

M

Is that why you're here?

G

What do you mean?

M

To give them permission to force-feed me.

G

Is that what you think? Do you think that's why I'm here?

M

You're a physician?

G

Yes.

M

Only the uniform is missing.

G

Sorry? (*pause*) I think we'll take a look at your hearing. (*He laughs a little, stands up, picks up a pair of earphones, and walks over to her.*) I'm just going to put these on you. (*short pause*) How's that? (*short pause*) Good, I hope. Good. You'll hear a number of separate sounds in your right ear. When you hear a sound just give me a sign. (*He looks at her. She doesn't say anything.*) Maybe you could lift your right hand or say "now" or just nod your head. Do you understand? (*pause*) Good. Terrific. (*He walks back to his chair, sits down, and pushes a button on a gadget on a table next to his desk.*)

M

Yes. (*reacting to the different sounds, from the lowest base tone to the highest*)

G

Excellent. (*pause*) Now you'll hear a number of sounds in your left ear. (*She reacts the same way as before. After a pause, he looks at the medical records.*) There doesn't seem to be any big changes from seven years ago. You don't seem to have any problems with the very high and the very low notes . . . but there might be a slight problem in the middle register. That's where the normal talking levels are . . . a slight but still obvious change.

M

In what ear?

G

Well, in both ears. (*short pause*) I mean, you're only thirty-three years old. Would you please stand up and lie down on the cot over there. I'm going to draw some blood and do the EKG and the EEG.

M

No.

G

Sorry?

M

I don't feel like it.

G

You don't feel like it? (*pause*) Okay. (*short pause*) Good. (*pause*) Terrific. (*short pause*) We might as well end everything here then. (*pause*) You can leave now.

M

Leave?

G

Yes. Sure. I'll call the guard.

M

Where?

G

Sorry?

M

Where am I supposed to go? (*short pause*) You said I could leave. (*short pause*) Where should I go?

G

Well . . . go back.

M

Go back?

G

Yes, to the ward . . . to the history books. (*laughs*) I'm sorry. (*short pause*) I'm sorry I laughed. That was impolite. But there's no reason for me to ask you to participate in something you don't want to participate in.

M

I'm not going to do or say anything until they turn off the light.

G

The light, what light?

M

The light in my cell.

G

What about it?

M

It's turned on.

G

So it's turned on. Why shouldn't it be?

M

Night and day. Year after year. Always. It's always turned on. It's never off. There's never any darkness. Ever. It's always turned on. The whole time. Do you understand?

G

Aha.

M

Do you understand?

G

Yes . . . I think so.

M

Do you understand what I'm telling you?

G

I think so.

M

There's no place in the cell where there's any less light. It doesn't help to close my eyes. They might as well cut my eyelids off. It seeps through even if I put a blanket or a pillow or a mattress over my face. It's there even if I wrap my head in a sheet. It's as bright as the sunlight in Crete in July.

G

I understand. . . . I must say it sounds rather unpleasant.

M

You really don't have to say that it sounds unpleasant. You don't think that it sounds unpleasant. You think it sounds great.

G

Why would I think that . . . that it's great?

M

Because you were the one who told them.

G

(*writes something on a piece of paper*) I'll bring it up. I'll mention it when I get a chance. I've made a note of it.

M

About what?

G

About remembering to mention it when I see them. That you suspect that I've told them to leave the light on day and night. More than that I can't do. (*pause*) I think I saw somewhere that you made several trips to Libya. Is that right? (*short pause*) Were you possibly thinking of that sunlight by mentioning Crete? The sunlight in Libya? Not the sunlight in Crete, but in Libya. Could that be it? (*short pause*) Well, it doesn't matter. It's of no importance. (*short pause*) I reacted because I, myself, visited Crete for three weeks in July, on vacation with my family. It was mostly for the culture, the landscape, the ancient ruins, the ravines . . . and, of course, the cave of the Minotaur. . . . We went there too. . . . Very interesting, very fascinating. And, thank God, there weren't as many Germans there as we had suspected. (*laughs*) We rented a car and drove

all over the island. (*short pause*) Well, that was that, now, let's see . . .
where were we?

M

What did your father do during the war?

G

My father? (*short pause*) He's dead.

M

What did he do during the war?

G

My father . . . he was . . . if we have to talk about him . . . during the war
he was, as so many others, ordered to take part in the war effort.

M

Was he a physician as well?

G

Yes, he was a physician.

M

Where was his practice located?

G

He died in 1951, when I was three years old.

M

Why don't you want to answer my question?

G

I think I answered your question.

M

I didn't ask when he died. I asked where his patients died.

G

I just mean that, for very obvious reasons, I don't have a lot of
information regarding the man who was my father, information one
should have about one's father. But since he passed away when I was
very young . . . I was just three years old. I didn't know him. I was a
child.

M

It's a moral obligation to find out what they did, and how much they enjoyed what they did.

G

Of course. Generally speaking. Absolutely. That is my view as well. We have to learn from history, from our past. Without knowing anything about our background we obviously grope in the dark. It goes without saying. Personally I haven't had the opportunity of digging as deeply into my past as I would have liked to, since studying to become a medical doctor, establishing a family life, and bringing up two children and such things basically have occupied all my time. There simply hasn't been enough time.

M

I've also studied.

G

Yes. (*short pause*) Didn't you study political science?

M

Isn't that why I'm here?

G

I would really like to continue with the medical checkup. (*pause*) Do you want to or not? (*long pause*) I had asked you why you aren't taking care of your personal hygiene any more.

M

There isn't anything personal any more.

G

I imagine there must be some personal integrity in spite of the situation one finds oneself in.

M

Don't you feel well?

G

Me?

M

Yes. How are you?

G

Fine. I'm fine. Why do you ask?

M

You're perspiring.

G

Really. (*short pause*) That's possible.

M

Aren't you aware of that?

G

What?

M

You're all wet from perspiration.

G

Well, that's possible. There's no air in here. The ventilation could have been better. (*short pause*) The room is very small.

M

Did you take a look at the chair?

G

What chair?

M

The one you're sitting in. Did you notice that you've moved the chair you're sitting in more and more to the left? Haven't you noticed that you're moving the chair you're sitting in more and more to the left, and you keep turning away from me when you're trying to talk to me, in a desperate effort to both be here and get away from here?

G

No, I don't think so.

M

I think so.

G

Why would I do that?

M

Because I have strong convictions and knowledge that pose a direct threat to your whole social and personal existence.

G

You? (*short pause*) Not at all. . . . On the contrary.

M

On the contrary? (*short pause*) Are you moving the chair because I lack the convictions and knowledge that pose a threat to your whole social and personal existence?

G

No . . . I mean . . . in what way do you mean that you would pose any threat to my social and personal existence? You're locked up. You're cut off. Completely isolated. You're being watched night and day. You're being watched as we speak. You'll never get out of here. Not alive any-way, as far as I can tell. Judging from everything, you'll die here. I will not. I'll leave here, let's say, in an hour. I'll never come back here.

M

In a little while you'll be sitting with your back facing me—and you'll fall apart.

G

You think so?

M

Absolutely.

G

We'll see.

M

How old am I?

G

What?

M

Don't you know how old I am?

G

Yes, I know how old you are. (*short pause*) How old are you?

M

Sixty-seven years old.

G

How old do you, yourself, consider yourself to be?

M

Sixty-seven years old. I've stopped menstruating. Is that normal?

G

Sixty-seven years old? Then I would think that it would be high time for that to happen. (*He unscrews the cap of his fountain pen and writes something on the pad in front of him.*) Gott . . .

M

Did you make a note of it?

G

What? That you've stopped menstruating at sixty-seven years of age?

M

That I'm sixty-seven years old. Did you write that down?

G

That you're telling me that you're sixty-seven years old? No, why would I do that? I know that you aren't sixty-seven years old. You're thirty-one years old. You are the same age as my wife. Obviously I know how old she is. Her name is Claire. Do you know her? Did you ever meet her?

M

Your wife?

G

Usually at this time of the day she drinks a glass of dry, white wine, a glass of Chardonnay, and is curled up in an easy chair in our living room watching the TV news hour. She says that she can't understand people like you. She thinks that you're simply revolting against your family.

How in the world would you have met her? The two of you do not move in the same circles.

M

I can see what you're thinking.

G

Really. Aha. (*short pause*) What?

M

You're thinking that you'd like to penetrate me.

G

Penetrate you? Why would I want to do that?

M

That's why you're talking about your "so-called" wife. (*short pause*) Is that what you want?

G

Actually, no, I don't. No.

M

Isn't that what you want?

G

What?

M

To penetrate me?

G

I'd like to continue with the examination. That's the only thing I want.

M

I don't want to talk to you anymore.

G

That's fine. I can examine you without us saying a word.

M

I want to talk to Willy Brandt.

G

I understand.

M

I want to talk to Willy Brandt, Helmut Schmidt, Kurt Waldheim, Henry Kissinger, and Richard M. Nixon. In that order. First of all Willy Brandt.

G

What do you want to discuss with Willy Brandt?

M

Talk about you. . . . . Are you married?

G

(*looking at her medical records*) It says here that you've made a request from the library for the book *Gravity and Grace* by the French, Catholic author Simone Weil.

M

Answer my question, fucking asshole.

G

Your question? (*short pause*) Which one?

M

You're crazy. I asked if you're married.

G

Yes, I'm married. I think I had mentioned that I had spent three weeks with my family on the Greek island of Crete. I think I had mentioned that I was there on vacation with my family. Talking about a family usually means that there is a husband and a wife. If a man says that he has been on vacation with his family, wherever they were, he usually means that he was on vacation with his wife, and of course with their children, if there are children. You are not going to provoke me. I'm not receptive to provocations. Recently I attended a course in how to react to provocations, however provoking they are. Nothing you say will make me react negatively. I'm capable of continuing my task regardless of how you act. It's meaningless for you to try. I just wanted you to know that.

M

I don't give a fuck about your wife and children, and you don't either.

G

That's true. That's correct.

M

It is?

G

That's to say . . . obviously I have to keep them out of the task I've been given to be able to perform the task as conscientiously and carefully as it should be done. Still, it is for their sake . . . for them to feel safe and secure . . . that we do what we have to do.

M

What did you write down?

G

I wrote "violin." (*short pause*) The word "violin."

M

Well, write whatever you want. Are you going to play the violin . . . with your children?

G

No, no, no. I don't play the violin. . . . Unfortunately I have no musical talent whatsoever. But you, you used to play the violin. You were a member of a string quartet in your youth, weren't you?

M

I don't remember. How would I remember that?

G

You don't remember that? Strange.

M

Yes, isn't it?

G

I don't think there's anyone who wouldn't remember that. To have been a member of a string quartet. (*short pause*) So, you really don't remember that?

M

No. Sorry. Something has happened to my memory.

G

Do you remember that you asked for a violin a couple of years ago? (*pause*) Did you get one?

M

Yes, I think so.

G

What?

M

That they gave me a violin.

G

Good. Did you play the violin?

M

No.

G

Why not?

M

Why do you ask about that?

G

I don't know. (*short pause*) Why didn't you play the violin?

M

Now I remember.

G

What?

M

Why I didn't play.

G

Well?

M

They had removed the strings.

G

On the violin? (*short pause*) All of them? All the strings?

M

Why would they have left one string if they removed all the others?

G

Well . . . maybe as a safety precaution . . . for reasons of safety. Maybe they wanted to prevent you from using the strings to make something you could use to hang yourself. Wasn't that what you were thinking? To escape your responsibility?

M

There are no sounds here. Not a sound. No sounds at all. I want to hear sounds.

G

What kind of sounds?

M

Simone Weil wasn't a Catholic.

G

Who? Simone Weil? (*short pause*) She wasn't?

M

She said that if there was a notice on the church doors stating "no entry" to everyone with an income above such and such an amount, quite low actually, she would leave the Catholic Church.

G

Aha. (*short pause*) Was she a communist?

M

She was Jewish. What else could she have been?

G

Do you identify with her?

M

Do you?

G

Do you?

M

Of course.

G

In what way?

M

That's the only thing one can do today in Germany, if one wants to feel like a decent human being. To feel shame for not being Jewish. The trains are still rolling toward the same stations. . . . You're a psychiatrist, aren't you?

G

Psychiatrist?

M

Nazi psychiatrist?

G

Should we agree that we keep to one subject at a time? Get rid of one subject then another. What makes you think that I'm a psychiatrist?

M

What do you like the most? Observe how people are being tortured, or do the torture yourself?

G

No, I'm not a psychiatrist. I'm a medical doctor. The fact is that my specialty is the illnesses of the heart. (*short pause*) Have you ever had any heart problems? Irregular heartbeat? Sudden strong pain? Do you exercise regularly? How's your sleep? How many hours do you sleep nightly?

M

I've to go to the bathroom.

G

Why?

M

I need to use the bathroom.

G

Why?

M

Why?

G

Just piss on the rug . . . Don't be embarrassed. I've seen everything. Bruckner gets 80 milligrams of Seconal every night. Otherwise he's just lying down on his cot screaming. He's incapable of accepting the reality he's in. Soon we'll have to give him a higher dosage—or stop medicating him completely. Right now he's in the shit room. It's called the shit room because that's where people are placed who are so traumatized from being in total isolation that they can't hold it in. They have completely lost control over their emotional and bodily functions. He's lying down naked on a cot covered with plastic. A guard is sitting on the other side of the bulletproof glass door watching him day and night, except when the guard reads the paper and drinks coffee. Of course it isn't the same guard watching him day and night. That would be much too stressful. There's a team of four men being responsible for sharing the twenty-four-hour duty. Would you be interested in seeing him? I mean, do you want to see the person lying on the cot—not the person watching him at this moment? It's possible that you might not recognize him, but they'll be able to tell you who he is. Well, of course, that's out of the question. You'll never see him. You'll never see him again, not alive, not as far as I can tell. Whatever happens later, in the afterlife, we have nothing to do with that. Anything else you want to know?

M

No. (*pause*) Yes.

G

Well . . . what's there to tell? (*short pause*) He was brought there about three weeks ago. It was a Sunday. Around lunchtime. The weather was beautiful. The sun was shining. He walked across the inner courtyard between two guards, dressed only in a big diaper. Of course, wearing handcuffs and foot chains as well. Are you interested in theater? Film? Religion? What kind of music do you want us to play for you in the loudspeakers? French Baroque music? Lully? Debussy? Should we ask one of the guards to read Corneille or Racine to you? France is a wonderful country. French culture. I love France. I go there regularly, at least once a year. Usually I spend at least two weeks of my vacation in France. My wife was born there. She comes from a small town called Chinon. In Chinon they produce a wine that's also called Chinon. A nice everyday wine. It's particularly good as a lunch wine, since it isn't very strong. Chinon is about twenty kilometers from Tours in Pays de Loire. The famous French painter Georges de La Tour is from Tours. I met her, my wife, when I was on a study trip with my law school class when I was twenty-two years old. Do you know who I am? (*pause*) Do you know who I am, you fucking cunt? (*pause*) I'm forty-three years old. I was just three years old when my father died, when the Second World War ended. I have two children. Two boys. I love them. They love me. Do you love me?

M

You?

G

Yes. Do you love me? Is the light bothering you?

M

In what way?

G

The light? (*short pause*) Is the light in your eyes? Do you want me to turn the lamp a little to the left or to the right?

M

No.

G

No? (*short pause*) Neither to the left nor to the right?

M

No.

G

What?

M

No . . . please turn it upwards a little.

G

Upwards? (*turns the lamp upwards*) Like this? Is this good?

M

I don't know.

G

Even more? (*turns the lamp a little more upwards*) Like this?

M

Thank you.

G

Is this good?

M

Yes, it's good. Thank you.

G

You're welcome. (*pause*) Where was I?

M

I don't know.

G

Me neither. (*pause*) I like this. I like it very much.

M

You do?

G

Yes. I like this. I do. What South American president promoted Augusto Pinochet in nineteen seventy-three to become chief of the Army?

M

Is that a medical question?

G

A medical question? Why?

M

You are a physician.

G

That's correct. I am. I am a physician. Are you *"virgo intacta?"*

M

No. I'm in Essen.

G

And your mother? Is she also in Essen?

M

I don't know . . . I haven't had any contact with her for a long time.

G

With your mother?

M

Yes.

G

Is she also *"virgo intacta?"*

M

Is that of any relevance?

G

Relevant of what?

M

For you.

G

For me everything is relevant. What would you prefer, if you had any choice in the matter, that I thrust my right index finger or my cock in your eye? (*short pause*) No answer? (*short pause*) You can't answer me, or you don't want to answer me? (*pause*) Then answer this question, maybe it'll be easier: What would you tell the children and the wife of the man whose death and maiming you carry the moral responsibility

for? Would you ask for forgiveness? (*short pause*) Maybe you've nothing to say? (*pause*) Do you want to take a short break?

M

Yes.

G

Excellent. (*pause*) How are you?

M

Fine, thank you.

G

Excellent. . . . Nice taking a break now and then. (*pause*) In confidence, I
can tell you that your father has written a letter to me.

M

I miss my hair.

G

Your father has written a personal letter to me. That's a little strange. I
don't know him. In the letter he talks about his faith. He believes in God.
He used to be a minister. Now he's retired.

M

Do you miss my hair?

G

This is the first time I've ever met you. I never met you before. I've been
curious to get to know more about you. I've almost had a longing to see
you and to talk to you. I think it could be described as a kind of longing.
Meaning, a longing to be alone with you and see you and talk to you.

M

Is this the first time you've met me?

G

First time? (*short pause*) Yes, absolutely it is. The first time. (*short
pause*) I'm sure of it. . . . Isn't it? Isn't this the first time?

M

I don't know.

G

It must be. (*short pause*) Isn't it?

M

I don't know. What are we doing now?

G

Now I'm going to ask you to go over to the cot over there and lie down on it. Then I want you to unbutton your blouse, so that I will be able to administer an EKG on you. Please get up and go over to the cot over there and lie down on it and unbutton your blouse. (*She stands up, walks over to the cot, lies down, and starts to unbutton her blouse. He stands up, takes out the EKG equipment, walks over to her, and opens up her blouse.*) Excellent. (*short pause*) This might feel a little cold. (*He places the electrodes on her chest.*) There. I think I've covered everything. (*He looks at her breasts.*) Excellent. (*short pause*) Now I just have to take some blood and check your blood pressure. Then we're almost done. This is going rather well, I think. Do they feel cold?

M

No. Do you want to touch me?

G

Touch you?

M

Yes. Do you want to?

G

Touch you? (*short pause*) What do you mean?

M

Isn't that what you want?

G

I don't understand.

M

Touch me. Caress me.

G

Was that what you meant?

M

Yes . . . do touch my breasts. Caress me.

G

That's something I can't do. That's impossible.

M

Hard. As hard as you can, you swine.

G

No. No. (*short pause*) That's inconceivable. Unthinkable. Not ethical. I couldn't possibly do that. Just think of my family. My sons. My colleagues. I would instantly lose my medical license. I could lose everything. They would see me. You would see me doing it. I would see me. It could never be undone. I would have to live with it for the rest of my life. I wouldn't be able to live with it. My sons wouldn't be able to live with it. My father would turn away from me. And rightly so. It would be like making love to an animal. You see, you're an animal. You're a criminal animal. I'm a human being. A human shouldn't fornicate with an animal. (*short pause*) Shall we continue? (*He removes the electrodes.*)

M

Yes. (*She sits up and buttons her blouse*)

G

Do you want to continue?

M

Yes. Of course.

G

You don't want to take a break?

M

No.

G

Then we'll continue. You can go back and sit in the chair. (*He waits. She sits down.*)

M

May I have a cigarette?

G

I'm sorry, I don't have any cigarettes. (*He drinks from a glass filled with water, which sits to the right of him.*) He's asking for permission to come and visit you.

M

Who is? (*short pause*) Your son?

G

No, your father. We're talking about your father. This whole time I've been talking about your father. Aren't you aware of that? I've tried, for a while now, to talk about your father. Not about my son. My son is nine years old. If everything is the way it's supposed to be, as it should be, if nothing unexpected has happened to him since I left him earlier today, he's probably in his bed sleeping by now. That's what he should be doing. Quietly asleep, feeling safe. Breathing without any effort. Why wouldn't he? Since he knows that his family is protecting him from all evil in this world. He knows that nothing will happen to him as long as his father dutifully and carefully does his job. A little white lamp, made of porcelain, is lit by his headboard. He's wearing blue-striped pajamas. He's sleeping on his left side, as he always does, with his legs curled up as if he was about to jump. On the floor below his bed is his big model train set. He inherited parts of the train set from his grandfather, who loved, truly loved, to relax playing with it the few times he visited the family on leave from his pressing work schedule. He has been playing with the trains all day. He put down the tracks, the trains, the station houses, the platforms, the German Shepherds, the soldiers, the guard rails lit by strong floodlights, and the people arriving on the trains in a large, shadowlike landscape. It looks so real one can't help being fascinated by it. It has its own reality. One is fascinated. Everything is the way it should be, except smaller. Tomorrow he'll continue playing the same game. There's one small detail that strikes me. . . . In some of the cars, once the trains have deposited their load, one can find small books by Goethe and Schiller, and small shoes and watches and wallets. . . . But, as I said before, right now he has left it standing there. Tomorrow he'll continue playing the game again. He knows all the train schedules and number of transports by heart. However complicated the planning is, it almost always seems to work. Everyone going to a destination arrives as planned, even if a part of the train might have to wait at the end terminal now and then, due to the fact that the deportation might take a little longer. I usually go into his room when I get home from work. Tired, weak, empty, burned out. Why? Because I've spent so much of my time with soulless people, people filled with pettiness, greed, and hunger for power. People who break down society with their intrigues and their jealousness. No one who hasn't experienced it can understand the difficulties I have to endure. After a while I can't even speak any longer. I can hardly open my mouth. Perspiration breaks out on my forehead and all over my body. It becomes hard for me to breathe naturally. After the interrogations I have to conduct with them, and the decisions I have to make, I notice that I have turned the chair I've been sitting in almost a full turn, in order to get away from them, trying to avoid entering their world. I'm completely exhausted. I drive home. I park the car under the big platan tree. It's raining lightly. You know that it's always raining in Kassel. I walk upstairs in our house. My wife is asleep. I go into the nursery. There my son is sleeping in his bed, not knowing anything about what he is soon to learn about the evil in this world. I sit down on his bed. I take his hand. I listen to his breathing. Quietly I say his name. I start to cry. I admit it. I cry violently, uncontrollably. I cry when I think of all the experiences he has ahead of him, experiences that very soon will push him out of his safe and secure little world that he's accustomed to. When I think of all the degrading and merciless events he'll be part of, just because he's getting older . . . well, that makes me cry. Who will he become? Who will change him into someone he isn't now? How many disappointments and deceits will he be forced to endure? Why does he have to experience all the cruelty the world is made of just to become a man? Why does he have to live?

M

Why?

G

Why is it necessary for them to live and die?

M

In Kassel?

G

In Kassel? (*pause*) No, not in Kassel. I don't think he'll remain in Kassel once he's grown up. I think he'll leave Kassel and live somewhere else.

M

Why?

G

I don't know. But I do admit that I cry when I think about it. But there's no other alternative. A son has to, sooner or later, leave his mother . . . and his father. (*short pause*) I'm sorry. (*short pause*) I only have a few more questions. . . . So, since we were talking about it . . . how does it feel to kill someone?

M

War. (*short pause*) There was a war.

G

How does it feel afterwards? (*short pause*) Tell me how it felt . . . feels, how it feels.

M

Empty.

G

Empty? Empty? How come?

M

Empty. (*short pause*) Was it all there is?

G

Was it all there is? Is that what you mean?

M

No?

G

Is that what it feels like? Was it all there is?

M

The first time . . . was it all there is, the first time?

G

Empty. Senseless. (*short pause*) Empty? (*short pause*) Maybe like after having sex?

M

I vomited.

G

Vomited?

M

Both times. (*short pause*) After both times.

G

Which one was the worst? (*short pause*) They say that it's usually worse for the girl. Women say that. (*short pause*) How old were you?

M

There was a war. I told you there was a war.

G

I mean . . . how old were you the first time you had sexual intercourse? How old were you the first time you showed your genitals to someone? Was he a professor at the University of Frankfurt teaching Sociology and Political Science? How old was he? (*short pause*) Strictly a routine question. You see, I have to ask these questions. I'm just a bureaucrat. I have no personal interest in your answers. Your answers don't mean anything to me. To me your answers don't matter at all. They go right through me. I don't even know what happens to your answers. How would I know? Did you like it?

M

Yes.

G

Did you like all the excitement around you, the attention, the focus on you, the photographers, the cameramen, the journalists, the police, the armored cars, the hunt, the loneliness, the fear, the hysteria, the desperation. . . . Did you like being hunted, exhausted, captured, chained . . . the undressing in public places, being taken away covered with blankets, like an expensive racehorse? Did you like the "line-ups," the trials, the verdicts, the isolation, the silence, the graves? Did you like dying?

M

There was a war.

G

My father has a bird farm, a chicken farm, in his country place, situated about thirty kilometers from Koblenz. Do you know how many chickens he has? He has five thousand chickens within an area of five hundred square meters. Do you know what that is? It's a concentration camp for chickens.

M

Your father?

G

Yes . . . my father.

M

You told me he was dead.

G

Who? (*short pause*) Who's dead?

M

Your father.

G

My father?

M

Your father. You said that he was dead.

G

Yes, he's dead. My father is dead. Your father is alive. My father died when I was about two years old. I'm sure I told you that. I'm talking about my Uncle Willi. He was like a father to me. When I see him I call him "father." He's seventy-two years old. He was the deputy to Edmund Heines in Breslau. His father whipped him hard for the smallest infraction. His brother fucked him regularly and without mercy, and his sister . . . his sister . . . I can't at this moment seem to remember her name. She owned a boarding house in a small town in the Mosel valley. During her active working life . . . she's a widow now . . . she always said that the young officers she socialized with in Munich were the most charming men she had ever met. The only thing she could think of when she thought of them was their incredible charm, and that it wasn't for her to stand in judgment of them. Charm like that isn't found anymore, she said; it belongs to a time long gone. Once, my father sold our Steinway piano in order to be able to buy a fur coat for his mistress. He forced me to start playing the violin when I was four years old. That's how I met my future wife, through my music. She was a violinist. The first time we met was in Chinon, in France, in the Loire Valley during a summer course for promising young musicians, in a beautiful little castle. However, these days we have no time for music. That is sad. We talk about it sometimes . . . how much we miss it, those moments when we used to make music together. Now we're much too busy. There isn't enough time. Not enough time for Beethoven. Your father is writing, wondering when he might see you. He's wondering how long it'll be before he can see you.

M

No.

G

No? He isn't?

M

I don't want to.

G

What is it you don't want to?

M

I don't want to see him.

G

No? (*short pause*) Am I the only one you want to see?

M

Yes. Just you.

G

You only want to see me?

M

Yes. Only you.

G

Even though I don't have any feelings for you?

M

Yes.

G

And never will have any feelings for you?

M

Yes.

G

Is that what attracts you to me?

M

What?

G

That I'll never have any feelings for you?

M

I don't know. (*pause*) Who are you?

G

Who am I?

M

Yes. Who are you?

G

Yes, who are we really . . . when everything is said and done?

M

What is said and done?

G

Maybe I don't know who I am, but I know where I am. I'm in my office. This is my office. These are my office furniture pieces. My lamp. My desk chair. My filing cabinet. My files. My notes. My papers. My photographs. The men you see in those photographs on the wall are my teachers. Those are my certificates and diplomas hanging behind me to the left. Over there. (*short pause*) The easy chair over there is also mine. It's from Italy. Black leather. Real leather. One can smell it when the weather changes. Almost like a human being. I can lie down in it. Like a human being. How do I do that? I just push the seat and it becomes a bed when I feel I have to stretch out, close my eyes, take a rest. Now and then I have to get away from everything and let my thoughts wander wherever they want. My work is horrible. Insurmountable. It never ends. There's no end to it. To cleanse the world. That takes a lot out of you. To make decisions regarding the quickest and most effective way, and also the most cost effective way, to make the world clean again. You can't really leave it when you go home at six. When you go home to your son. (*short pause*) That's right. I have a son. Soon he'll be seven years old. He's a normal, intelligent, patriotic boy. I've brought him up to be a good and loyal citizen. I encourage him to take part in both sports and cultural activities, and to take an interest in history. His country's history. Soon we'll have been a democracy for thirty years. That's something terrific. Where did it take us? Plenty of space for people like you, freedom for people like you. . . . Terrorism. (*short pause*) I hope he'll never treat me with the kind of brutality and cruelty that you're showing your father. You don't even want to see him. Don't you understand how this has affected him and his family? He isn't young anymore. How could he be? Since you're thirty-one years old. He could pass away any day now. The only thing holding him together and that gives him some solace is his faith. His strong faith. He's a minister. He believes in God. I also believe in God. I think God is with me right now. I think that God is speaking through me, in this moment, as I am completing this difficult task. With God I have no freedom. Believing in God makes you do what's right and good. That's why we don't suffer doubts or compunctions. Do you know what your father writes? Your father writes that he recently started a collection of funds to be used for the care of your teeth. Your teeth? What's wrong with your teeth? Are you losing your teeth? How many have you lost? How many do you have left? (*pause*) I'm asking you how many you have left. Teeth. In your mouth. (*short pause*) Don't you think I expect answers to my questions? Do you think I'm asking questions I don't expect to be answered? Do you really think that? Do you think I like wasting my time? (*short pause*) Open your mouth. (*short pause*) I guess I have to count your teeth myself. (*She opens her mouth.*) Thank you. (*He bends down and counts her teeth with his fountain pen.*) Your breath smells rotten. You smell like cunt. (*short pause*) Ten teeth. (*short pause*) I guess that's enough. Why are you causing trouble? Don't you know there's a war?

M

I want more vegetables.

G

More vegetables? There's a war . . .

M

When I ask for water I get Coca-Cola.

G

Coca-Cola is an excellent beverage. It's one of the world's most frequently sold products. We've recently lost a world war in order to have the freedom to drink Coca-Cola. Do you know where you are?

M

Yes.

G

Where are you?

M

In your office. (*short pause*) Am I not?

G

You're the one answering questions. Not me. What day is it today?

M

Sunday.

G

What date?

M

The twenty-third . . . March twenty-third.

G

March?

M

Yes, March twenty-third, nineteen seventy-four.

G

Not March. (*short pause*) It's July.

M

July?

G

Of course. July seventeenth. It's July seventeen, nineteen ninety-two. It's summer. Not spring.

M

Summer?

G

The apex of summer. Thirty-six degrees Celsius in the shade. It's been above thirty degrees for almost two weeks. Our climate is almost tropical. The temperature doesn't go below twenty degrees even during the night. That means the climate is tropical. The landscape is already brown and parched. The wheat fields have been harvested and the mountains and the valleys are shimmering from heat in the far haze. The water is receding in the riverbeds. The factories are closed, as are the schools. The industrial vacations began last week. The autobahns are blocked by vacationers on their way to the French Riviera or to Italy. There have been problems getting through the Brenner Pass and the tunnel. Delays. The people who don't have the money for vacations are seeking shade under the Linden trees and the Birch trees in different parks. The sun is just setting . . . pale, pink light in the white haze. It's almost night time. Should we continue?

M

Kill me.

G

Should we continue to talk about your father?

M

Why don't you kill me?

G

Kill you?

M

Yes.

G

Sorry.

M

I'm begging you.

G

To kill you?

M

Yes.

G

How would I do that?

M

You're a physician.

G

I am?

M

That's what you told me.

G

That I'm a physician?

M

Yes. . . . Why don't you give me some pills so that I can die?

G

Of course I could, but I'm not allowed to do that. Our country's laws do not allow for capital punishment. You'll be in here for another twenty years. Where were we? Yes, what are the highways in Germany called where you can drive as fast as you can? (*short pause*) Did you hear what I said?

M

What did you say?

G

I said, "What are the highways called where you can drive your vehicle as fast as you can?" (*short pause*) Did you understand the question?

G
M

Yes.

G

Then answer me. What are they called?

M

They are called autobahns.

G

They are called autobahns. (*short pause*) Do you remember when you were twelve years old and were traveling by car on the autobahn with your father, who was a minister, and was driving, sitting next to your mother in the front seat, and with two of your siblings? A third sibling— an older brother—had stayed home that summer in order to better his knowledge of Latin. You traveled through Germany to spend your vacation in Venice. Do you remember that?

M

No.

G

You were twelve years old.

M

I was? Twelve years old?

G

You had cut off your long hair. You had short hair. You had the same haircut as Audrey Hepburn.

M

Who?

G

Audrey Hepburn. An American movie star. She was in "Roman Holiday." Her leading man was the American star Gregory Peck. Was it during that vacation-week in Venice that you, for the first time, came in contact with Jewish, Marxist thinking? Was that when you started to read Marxist literature? Did you read Franz Fanon, Jean Paul Sartre, Cohn-Bendit, Regis Debray, Georg Lukacs?

M

No.

G

Didn't you read Georg Lukacs? (*short pause*) Why?

M

I was twelve years old.

G

You could read.

M

I was twelve years old. I read magazines. I was sunbathing. I had a white bathing suit. I fell in love with a boy.

G

Was he a Marxist?

M

He was seventeen years old.

G

The boy you fell in love with. I asked if he was a Marxist?

M

I was twelve. We stayed in Fiesole . . . not in Venice. It was in Florence.

G

Florence? Are you sure?

M

It wasn't Venice. It was Florence. Of course I'm sure of it.

G

You would have remembered if you'd been there. The Donatello Museum?

M

Yes, I think so.

G

How did you like it?

M

I was twelve years old.

G

Do you know when and where he was born?

M

I was twelve years old.

G

Do you know when he died?

M

I was twelve years old.

G

Excellent. (*short pause*) Then I don't have any more questions.

M

What did you say?

G

I have no more questions. We're done. The medical examination is completed.

M

It is?

G

Yes. We're done. I'll just ask the guard to come and get you.

M

Aha . . . what about you?

G

Me?

M

What are you going to do? Are you going home?

G

Home? I have no home. Just as you have no home. We have no homes. Neither one of us will return to a home. There's no home for us to return to. That, which we usually call a home, however temporary or defective it might be, is today just the bottom of what once was a lake somewhere. Just sand and dried clay. A desert. Hard and naked. Soundless and cold as the universe itself. Horrific. Without end. Without life. Without feelings. Without memory. Dead. Didn't you know that? By the way, one of your friends hanged himself in his cell yesterday.

M

No. (*pause*) Who? (*pause*) Who?

G

Unfortunately I can't tell you that. You understand, don't you?

THE END

TERMINAL 3

Characters

SHE, in her early twenties

HE, in his early twenties

WOMAN, in her forties

MAN, in his forties

GUARD, an older man

The setting is a hospital waiting room.

A *big room with no people and nondescript hospital furniture. It is very dark. Slowly the light gets brighter.*

                              HE
Is this it?

                              SHE
I don't know.

                              HE
Is this where we were? (*silence*) Could this be it?

                              SHE
I told you I don't know.

                              HE
Yeah.

                              SHE
How would I know?

                              HE
There's no one here.

                              SHE
I don't know anything.

                              HE
Since there isn't anyone to ask.

                              SHE
I don't know anything anymore.

                              HE
Fucking strange. (*silence*) I don't recognize anything . . .

                              SHE
Why don't you ask someone.

                              HE
Who?

SHE

Those who were out there . . .

HE

My God, it could happen any moment. (*short pause*) They told us to come here . . .

MAN

This is where . . .

SHE

Then I guess it's here.

HE

. . . and wait. (*silence*) Didn't they say that?

MAN

This is the same place.

WOMAN

What? (*turns around*)

MAN

The same place we were long ago . . . same hallway. We were here. We were in this waiting room. Fucking strange.

SHE

There's someone sitting there.

WOMAN

Isn't there anyone here?

MAN

Or a place just like it.

WOMAN

Where are we supposed to go now?

MAN

It's the same waiting room. I'm sure of it. I recognize the windows . . . these tall windows . . . and the furniture. Same furniture . . . placed in the same way. . . .

WOMAN

How could that be?

MAN

Because I remember. . . . Over there, that's where we were waiting. We were sitting and waiting over there. . . . You don't forget those things . . . even though it was long ago.

WOMAN

Isn't anyone working here?

MAN

I guess they use the same kind of furniture everywhere. Cheaper that way.

SHE

Maybe it's just pee.

HE

We'll have to wait here . . . for our turn.

SHE

Couldn't you come up with something better?

HE

What? (*short pause*)   What do you mean by that?

SHE

Forget it . . . (*silence*)

HE

Do you have pain?

SHE

No.

HE

No.

SHE

I have nothing.

HE
I have your bag here . . . if you need anything. (*silence*) Do you need anything?

SHE
No, thanks.

HE
Sure?

SHE
No, what would that be?

HE
Well, I don't know.

SHE
It's broken. I want to get rid of it.

HE
Emma. (*silence*)

SHE
I just want to get it over with.

HE
What?

SHE
I want to be the one I was before.

HE
Yes, but . . .

SHE
I want to be like the one I am.

HE
How?

SHE
But I can't. (*silence*)

WOMAN
Isn't there anyone here?

MAN
Doesn't seem like it.

WOMAN
Isn't that strange? (*silence*) Isn't it strange that no one is here?

MAN
Yes, it's . . . maybe it's strange. It's late.

WOMAN
That there isn't a guard here or something . . . anyone could just walk in.

MAN
We don't know that.

WOMAN
What?

MAN
There will be someone here soon, we hope.

WOMAN
No . . . I sort of hope that no one will show up. (*silence*) If no one comes, then maybe it isn't him, but somebody else.

MAN
Yes. (*silence*)

HE
They are waiting too.

SHE
Who?

HE
The people over there. . . . They came in when we came.

SHE
No, they came later. But they're really old.

HE

They are?

SHE

Can't you see that?

HE

They aren't that old. He isn't, anyway.

SHE

Don't look at them.

HE

Why not?

SHE

They'll know we're talking about them.

HE

This is so typical, having to wait when such big things are happening.

WOMAN

At least they could've had a few candles . . . some lit candles.

MAN

But this is just the waiting room.

WOMAN

Something, anyway.

HE

I think I know him. I guess I've seen him somewhere. Maybe he lives in the neighborhood.

WOMAN

Do you think we're in the right place?

MAN

Yes, we are. They told us to go to the building with a big C.

WOMAN

So, is that where we are?

MAN

Yes.

WOMAN

Are you sure?

MAN

No, I'm not sure. I'm not sure of anything; there isn't anything I'm sure of. The only thing I'm sure of is that there is a C, that there's a big C above the door. That I'm absolutely sure of. We both saw it. You were the one who saw it first. You were the one who told me.

WOMAN

Was it really a C?

MAN

Yes, there was a C above the door that we entered. A big fucking C. I'm sure of that. Everything else I'm not sure of.

WOMAN

Was it a C?

HE

I love you.

SHE

Okay.

MAN

No, it's a big fucking broken O.

WOMAN

Maybe it is.

HE

I'll come and pick you up when it's over, and then we'll walk home.

SHE

Walk?

HE

Yes . . . I'll carry him home.

SHE

Maybe I won't be able to walk home.

HE

Then we'll get a cab. But it seems silly to take a cab home, since we live so close by . . . just a few hundred yards.

SHE

At least a mile.

HE

Well, I'm just talking.

SHE

Is that something we have to decide right now?

HE

Nooo.

SHE

I feel anxious just thinking about what I should do. My life is so fucking planned out anyway.

HE

No, you don't have to. We don't have to decide anything.

SHE

We haven't even decided what to name him.

HE

No. (*short pause*)   But I think we'll know when he comes out.

SHE

Or she?

HE

I think we should call him John-John.

SHE

No, anything but that.

(*pause*)

HE

I think he'll say "Hello, my name is John-John" when he comes out. "What's your name?"

WOMAN

They sure are talking a lot. (*silence*)

HE

(*quietly*) And then we could move down to the house.

SHE

What did you say?

HE

(*more loudly*) I was just thinking that later on we could move down to the house. We'll pack up and put things in order, and then we'll drive down to our home. . . . And then we'll have the whole summer to make the house beautiful. We'll paint and put in new floors, eat in the garden, and spend whole days on the beach with him. Hell, I just long to get away from here, long to get in the car and leave all this, to get away from here.

SHE

It was stinking of seaweed.

HE

So what?

MAN

Do you remember when we . . . (*pause*)

SHE

Why don't you go home for now.

HE

What?

SHE

Yes, go.

HE

Go home?

SHE

Yes, if you want to . . . If you'd like to go home and rest for a while.

HE

Why would I like to do that?

SHE

I just thought that then you wouldn't have to sit here. You might just want to go home and rest for a while.

HE

No, I want to be here with you.

SHE

You never know how long it'll take. Maybe it won't happen until tomorrow.

HE

No, I want to be with you. Of course I want to be with you. I don't want to go home. I want to be here with you. But I do have some things I have to do.

SHE

You can't do anything anyway . . . not right now, anyway.

HE

You know I want to be here. Why do you say such strange things?

SHE

I know you want to go home.

HE

Why do you say that?

SHE

Because I can feel it.

HE

No, I don't want to go home.

SHE

I can feel that you think this is really tough.

HE

I don't think so at all. That's what you think. As usual you're projecting on me. The way you always do.

SHE

I don't have the strength for this.

HE

Me neither. (*silence*) Wait . . . I want to be here with you. That's the only thing I want. Don't you understand that?

MAN

Let's wait a little longer.

WOMAN

What else is there to do? Did you drive here?

MAN

No, I took a cab. (*silence*)

SHE

If something happens I guess they'll call you.

HE

No.

SHE

For your sake, I mean.

HE

You know I want to be part of it.

SHE

Yes. (*silence*) Mia said she'd be here later.

HE

Aha. Did you talk to Mia?

SHE

I just wanted to tell her that it was time.

HE

What the fuck, I'm the one who'll become a dad, not Mia.

SHE

I just wanted her to know.

HE

Sure. (*Silence, as "She" looks at a big brown photograph hanging on the wall.*) What is that?

SHE

I don't know . . . It looks like something terrible.

HE

(*He stands up and goes over to the picture.*) What is it?

SHE

Is it a foot?

HE

It's an x-ray of a little foot, a foot of a child, a child's foot with a big, rusty nail right through it.

SHE

Is that the nail, that dark thing?

HE

If it's a nail it should be light. Yes. It must be really old. (*silence*)

MAN

Don't you remember?

WOMAN

No.

MAN

Don't you remember that we were here?

WOMAN

I don't want to remember . . . not right now.

MAN

Anyway, it was here we were nineteen years ago. It looks exactly the same. It's as if nothing has changed. Only us. We used to live in that renovated apartment across the street, around the corner. The one that was so expensive, once they had renovated it. We lived on the top floor. The sixth floor. You were afraid to go out on the balcony. We looked right in here from our balcony.

WOMAN

That was just a French door with a railing.

MAN

Yes, but we weren't going to live there very long. (*silence*) Who was that?

WOMAN

Who?

MAN

There was someone over there.

WOMAN

Really?

MAN

Someone was over there. I thought I saw a man over there, at the end of the corridor.

HE

Someone was there.

WOMAN

Who?

MAN

I don't know. He disappeared. (*silence*) Should I go over there and ask?

WOMAN

No, don't.

MAN

No.

HE

I wonder what they are doing here. (*pause*) The couple sitting over there. (*pause*) Maybe they're somebody's parents. They're too old to be . . .

MAN

Should I ask, you think?

WOMAN

Yes, why don't you. (*silence*) It says it over there. (*silence*) Above the door. It says what it is.

MAN

What does it say? I couldn't find my glasses.

HE

What does it say?

WOMAN

Chamber for Family Members.

MAN

Chamber?

WOMAN

Yes.

MAN

May I borrow your glasses?

WOMAN

I don't have any. I left them in my office. Yes, I guess that's where we're supposed to go. That's where he is.

MAN

I can't see without my glasses.

WOMAN

Well, that's what it says.

MAN

Aha . . . Chamber for Family Members. (*silence*)

HE

Fuck, they're looking at us.

(*pause*)

SHE

Who?

HE

The people over there . . . There aren't any others.

WOMAN

Why are they looking at us?

MAN

Who? (*short pause*) Oh, they.

WOMAN

The couple over there.

MAN

Well, what else is there to look at?

WOMAN

I was just wondering what they're doing here.

MAN

I don't know.

WOMAN

They aren't that old.

MAN

That's what I said before.

WOMAN

Like us.

MAN

Like us. No, they aren't that old.

WOMAN

Maybe they're . . . maybe it's someone they know.

MAN

Yes. (*short pause*) How awful.

WOMAN

Maybe a friend or a sibling.

MAN

Sure. How terrible. (*short pause*) It could be the parents . . . one of the parents.

WOMAN

But they're so young . . . they're so young. . . . She looks like eighteen or nineteen.

MAN

Well, I don't know. I guess it depends on . . . if it's a . . . it could be a small child, I guess. (*silence*)

WOMAN

I don't know if I can . . .

MAN

What did you say?

WOMAN

I don't know if I'll be able to make it.

MAN

No, me either.

WOMAN

No.

MAN

But we have to.

WOMAN

Yes. (*silence*) Maybe it's somebody else.

MAN

Yes.

WOMAN

Maybe it isn't him. Maybe it's somebody else.

MAN

Yes.

WOMAN

I don't want to know.

MAN

No. (*He takes her hand.*)

WOMAN

I don't want to . . .

HE

Good that your mother will be coming in. Then she and I can put things in order before you two come home. We'll have time to make it nice for you to come home. Right now there's a real mess at home.

SHE

Are you saying that my stuff is making a mess? We're moving, so what does it matter?

HE

Yes, but . . .

SHE

How long have we been here?

HE

I don't know . . . maybe fifteen minutes.

SHE

It seems like weeks.

HE

They must know we're here. They haven't forgotten about us. They couldn't do that to us.

WOMAN

Do you think that they've forgotten about us?

MAN

Seems like it. That's what it seems like.

WOMAN
Yes, that's what it seems like.

HE
Maybe after a while we could go somewhere. Take a vacation. Go to Turkey or Crete or wherever, where the sea is warm. Sometimes the water gets warm in April or May already. Maybe we could find a cheap trip, a charter trip, and go away for a week or ten days.

SHE
How could we do that?

HE
There are cheap trips right now. There aren't that many traveling this time of the year.

SHE
You can't go anywhere with a newborn.

HE
No, not right now. Later.

MAN
It was nineteen years ago. Is it really nineteen years?

SHE
No, I don't want to think about it.

HE
No. Later. You don't have to think about it now. In a couple of months. Maybe in September.

SHE
No, it won't work. I can't.

HE
Maybe he could stay with your mother while we're away. Just for that short time.

SHE
No. I've got to get back to work.

HE

Work? Work? What do you mean?

SHE

Yes, I have to.

HE

What the hell do you mean by that?

SHE

They already asked if I could start next month.

HE

Next month?

SHE

May 1. The first week in May. I'm happy that someone is asking for me.
That someone wants me.

HE

The hell you can.

SHE

Why can't I? If I can travel, I might as well work. It's a lot more fun
working than going on some fucking charter vacation.

HE

What the hell, I thought you wanted to stay at home.

SHE

I'll be home for five weeks, almost six weeks.

HE

I don't get it. It's fucking crazy.

SHE

I want to get going as soon as possible, so that I'll feel normal again. So
that I'll be myself again.

HE

Yes, but . . . I think it's much too soon.

SHE

Not for me.

HE

For him or her. You've got to understand that.

SHE

I feel so cut off from everything. I'm cut off from the world and from myself, too. I don't know what's going on. I'm not in touch with myself. I'm like a stranger that I don't know, who's doing things that I normally don't do. It's as if I was cut off from my neck down.

HE

Yes, I know. You've told me that. Many times.

SHE

It doesn't help, whatever I say. You still don't understand.

HE

No. But I'm trying.

SHE

I don't understand myself.

HE

What?

SHE

What's happening. I don't understand what's happening.

HE

Couldn't you wait until after Christmas, anyway?

SHE

It's like watching a horror movie without sound and not understanding what they are doing, even though I'm part of it. . . . I want to get my life going again.

MAN

You can't have candles in a waiting room.

WOMAN

In churches they have them.

MAN

In churches, yes.

WOMAN

A church is like a waiting room, isn't it? (*silence*) They could have something that showed that . . .

MAN

People come and go here all day long.

WOMAN

So, where are they? (*silence*) There isn't a single human being here . . . except those poor people over there. Those two over there.

SHE

Are you leaving?

HE

No . . . I just wanted to stand up.

SHE

You can go home if you like.

HE

No, I said.

SHE

Since we live so close by. (*silence*)

HE

I told you that I'm staying.

WOMAN

We're waiting and waiting.

MAN

Yes.

WOMAN

That's what we did then, too.

MAN

Yes, what the hell else can we do?

WOMAN

We were waiting an unusually long time that time. (*silence*) Maybe it's somebody else.

MAN

Yes.

WOMAN

Maybe it's not him at all.

MAN

No.

WOMAN

Maybe it isn't Elias.

MAN

No.

WOMAN

Maybe it's someone who looks just like him.

MAN

But they called you. Why would they call you, if it wasn't the right . . .

WOMAN

They could be wrong. There could be a misunderstanding.

MAN

How?

WOMAN

A simple mistake.

MAN

How could that be?

WOMAN

I don't know. I'm just saying that . . . until . . . until we know.

MAN
Yes.

WOMAN
I don't know anything.

MAN
No, I'm just trying to . . . I'm trying to reach for some hope . . . something to . . . to hope for.

WOMAN
I talked to him just the other day.

MAN
You did?

WOMAN
Yes, a few days ago.

MAN
I didn't know that.

WOMAN
I called him, because it had been so long since I had heard from him.

MAN
What did he say? (*silence*) Did he seem depressed? Worried?

WOMAN
No, not at all. On the contrary. I hadn't heard him sound so happy in a long while. . . . He was joking . . .

MAN
About what? What did you talk about?

HE
I love you.

SHE
Yes.

(*pause*)

WOMAN

There was something really silly that we both laughed at. . . . I felt happy afterwards. When we were through talking, everything felt light. I usually feel happy afterwards. When the conversation is over.

HE

Someone's coming.

MAN

(*stands up*) Someone is coming.

WOMAN

Oh, no.

(*Guard comes in*)

MAN

Should we ask?

("*Woman*" *is sitting quietly*)

HE

Well, hello. Hello

GUARD

Are you the people who were supposed to be here?

SHE

Yes, I think so.

HE

Yes . . . that's what they said out there.

SHE

That we should come here.

HE

We've been sitting here waiting. Her water broke.

GUARD

Well, I've been very busy.

HE

Yes, where are we supposed to go?

GUARD

I thought you were older. That's what I thought.

HE

Older? Why?

GUARD

Well, maybe you're siblings or friends.

HE

No, we're married.

GUARD

Married? To each other?

HE

Yes, we've been married for almost a year.

MAN

(*comes up to them*) Hello . . . excuse me.

HE

Yes, isn't this where it is?

MAN

I just wanted to ask one thing, but I can wait.

GUARD

So, you're the people who were supposed to come here?

MAN

Yes . . . I don't know . . . I think so.

GUARD

You're here for an identification, right?

MAN

Yes, a boy.

GUARD

Yes, a young man.

MAN

Yes. Yes, that's us.

WOMAN

We don't know if it is . . .

GUARD

I was beginning to wonder what happened to you.

MAN

We've been waiting here.

GUARD

Well, I was in there, in the office.

WOMAN

We've been . . . waiting in here.

MAN

Is it a man . . . a young man?

GUARD

He, who was brought in this morning? Yes, he isn't that old.

MAN

He's nineteen years old.

WOMAN

Twenty.

MAN

Yes, twenty.

WOMAN

He was twenty in March, the nineteenth of March.

MAN

Blond. Very thin.

WOMAN

He's twenty years old.

MAN

He has blond hair. Very blond.

HE

Excuse me, but we were really here first.

GUARD

Yes, just a moment. Well, I haven't looked at him very carefully.

MAN

Did he . . . does he have blond hair?

GUARD

Yes.

HE

What the hell is this?

SHE

Take it easy. Easy.

GUARD

I haven't had the time to look at his hair color, what color his hair is.

WOMAN

Elias is tall and thin.

HE

We really were here first.

MAN

Yes. He turned twenty in March.

GUARD

Well I can't tell you very much. Better that you see for yourself.

HE

You could give birth any moment.

                         MAN
Yes, of course.

                          HE
What will you do then?

                        GUARD
I just received and registered the body when the police brought him in
this morning.

                         MAN
Is he hurt?

                        WOMAN
He was thinking of applying to a university to study education this fall.
. . . But first he wanted to take a year off to travel . . . to Australia.

                         MAN
Australia?

                        GUARD
Australia.

                          HE
What about us?

                         MAN
I didn't know that.

                        GUARD
Yes, maybe we should . . . Follow me and we'll find out if it's the right
person. Not until then can we be sure.

                         MAN
What was he going to do there?

                          HE
Excuse me . . .

                        GUARD
Yes?

HE

Yes excuse me, but I just wanted to ask if this is the maternity ward?

GUARD

If this is what?

HE

The maternity ward. Where people give birth.

GUARD

Oh, that. No, this is the waiting room . . .

HE

For what?

GUARD

Is that where you're going?

HE

Yes, my wife is about to give birth. They told us to come here.

GUARD

Yes, the maternity ward is over there, it's the other corridor, to the left.
The left corridor looking from this direction.

HE

Downstairs in the reception they told us to come here.

GUARD

Well, well . . . it's the other corridor, over there, where you see the doors.

HE

Over there?

GUARD

Straight ahead, and then to the left.

HE

Okay. (*silence*)

GUARD

Do you understand?

HE

I hope so.

GUARD

(*short pause*) Just go over there and ask.

HE

All right. Thank you.

GUARD

You see, once this was a separate building, but now the entrance is the same for both. But it's really two different buildings.

HE

Well, that's smart, I think.

GUARD

This is a different ward . . . but that's not easy to know.

HE

It doesn't say anything anywhere.

GUARD

No, there's just a letter above the doors.

HE

Okay.

GUARD

The other one, that's over there.

HE

But it's so dark over there.

GUARD

Yes, but there's always someone there.

HE

Okay. Thank you. Thank you very much.

GUARD

You're welcome.

MAN

That's what I said. It's the same place we were then.

GUARD

No, not at all.

MAN

Nineteen years ago.

GUARD

That's a different ward. This is the . . .

MAN

No, it wasn't.

GUARD

What?

MAN

No.

HE

Honey . . . Emma

SHE

Dear . . .

HE

Honey . . .

GUARD

Hope he'll find what he's looking for now.

MAN

Yes.

WOMAN

What are we supposed to do?

SHE

What did he say?

HE

We're supposed to go over there. Turn left over there.

SHE

So, then it isn't here. That's what I said.

HE

It's the same entrance, but we should've turned left instead.

SHE

But it's so dark.

HE

That's what he said.

SHE

Are you sure?

HE

Yes, I am. I asked him, didn't I?

SHE

But there's no one there.

HE

We don't know that, do we?

SHE

It's pitch black over there.

HE

Of course someone is there. Hell, people give birth all the time.

SHE

Why don't you go and ask him again.

HE

I already asked him.

SHE

Who?

HE

The guy who was here. (*silence*) Let's go.

SHE

It's so quiet. (*Silence, as she puts her hands on her stomach.*) In here.

HE

How's that?

SHE

It's so quiet. . . . I don't feel anything.

HE

But hurry up then. Are you in pain?

WOMAN

I don't know if I'll be able to handle this.

MAN

I can go. . . . Do you want me to do it?

WOMAN

No.

MAN

Wait here, then . . .

GUARD

No, this isn't easy. It's never easy. In a way it's even worse when they're so young.

MAN

Why don't you stay here?

GUARD

There are so many young ones these days. There seems to be more and more of them. . . . They aren't even . . . they're children. One would think that it would be the old ones. There are so many lonely, young people who are rotting away in their apartments.

MAN

Sure.

GUARD

It's hard to forget them.

WOMAN

No, I can't . . .

MAN

No.

WOMAN

I don't want to be left alone out here. . . . That I don't like.

GUARD

Maybe you'd like to wait a little while before . . .

MAN

No.

HE

Emma.

(*"She" slowly stands up and walks over to "Woman," "Man," and "Guard."*)

WOMAN

I know . . . I knew.

GUARD

Would you like me to turn on some music?

MAN

No, why?

GUARD

Some people want it, some people like that. What kind of music do you like?

MAN

No. (*"She" and "Woman" are facing each other. "Woman" looks at her, but "She" looks past her, is looking through her. "Woman" touches the breasts of the young woman, "She," and is softly holding the breasts.*) Emma . . . what are you doing?

WOMAN

I gave birth to a child. We had a child. Then we divorced. We should never have had a child. I was the one who left. One day I left. Elias was two years old then.

MAN

Emma . . . come now.

WOMAN

We should never have had one. I didn't want a child. But I had one.

MAN

Emma, you're talking to a stranger.

HE

Emma, what are you doing?

SHE

I'm just going to the bathroom.

GUARD

Over there. One of those doors.

(*"Woman" sits down. "She" leaves.*)

GUARD

Well, please follow me.

WOMAN

Everyone's leaving.

MAN

(*takes her hand*) Emma, come now.

WOMAN

I'm the only one left. (*silence*)

(*A body covered with a sheet is on a stretcher in the middle of the room. "He" enters the room, with the lighting making it appear as if "He" is in another room, where "She" is sitting on the bed.*)

SHE

Hello.

HE

Hello.

SHE

Hello.

HE

It's me. How are things? (*silence*) Are you sitting up?

SHE

Yes.

HE

(*sits down next to her, takes her hand*) How's it going? How are you?
You smell so good.

SHE

Tired.

HE

Of course you are. (*holds her*) That's not very strange. This is the biggest
thing that could ever happen. What a night, it's been an historical night.
(*silence*) Well, great. Feeling a little better?

SHE

Yes, I guess.

HE

Yes. Soon you'll be coming home.

SHE

Yes, but not today. (*silence*)

HE

It's a beautiful day. . . . Seventy degrees. I'm sure you feel the spring in
the air. The air is so clear, crystal clear. Makes one feel like playing soccer. (*pause*) But I'll have to wait until he gets a little bigger. For now
he'll just be a goalie.

SHE

They want you to sit up as soon as possible.

HE

And that's what you're doing. How do you feel?

SHE

I told you that I don't know. I don't know how I'm supposed to feel.

HE

No.

SHE

They never told me that it would hurt so much. They never did.

HE

No, it didn't say that in the book.

SHE

I thought I'd die. I almost did.

HE

You smacked me.

SHE

I did?

HE

Yes, you were hurting so much that you hit me. Smacked me right in my face. (*silence*)

SHE

I didn't mean to.

HE

No, that's all right. That's not why I said it. . . . I brought you this . . . (*shows her a bouquet of flowers and a bottle of champagne*) and then I brought a couple of books and magazines, if you'd like to read.

SHE

Thank you. Do they smell?

HE

Should I put them here?

SHE

I don't feel like reading.

HE

No, not now, later. Should I put them here? (*silence*)

SHE

Did you buy them downstairs?

HE

Yes. Does it matter where I bought them?

SHE

Did you buy them downstairs?

HE

I looked at him . . . I held him. . . . He was so light. . . . Like embracing air.

SHE

He's supposed to sleep.

HE

Before I came to you. Yes, he's asleep.

SHE

You can't wake him up.

HE

No. I was just looking at him. He's looking so good. He has little, fine hair on his shoulders and right between his shoulder blades. But they said that it would disappear.

SHE

I know. I'm not supposed to drink alcohol if I'm nursing.

HE

You could probably have one little drink now and then.

SHE

No. We don't want to make him into alcoholic, do we?

HE

What about it? His grandfather was an alcoholic.

SHE

That's right.

HE

So we have a boy. It's a boy, after all.

SHE

That's what you wanted, wasn't it? (*makes a grimace*)

HE

With blue eyes. (*pause*) Are you hurting?

SHE

Only when I move my body. . . . (*He laughs.*) What was so funny about that?

HE

No, no. Nothing. (*long pause*) It made me think of a story, a guy told me a story last night. There was this man who'd been tied to a tree by some natives somewhere in Africa. No, two men, two white guys . . . this happened a long time ago . . . who were tied to a pole. Then the natives ran spears right through their bodies, and one of them cried and screamed and howled in pain, but the other guy didn't show shit. Then the one who was screaming and howling asked the other one if he was in pain. Only when I laugh, he said.

SHE

Aha.

HE

That's why I was laughing.

SHE

Yes . . . I feel like I've had a spear going through my body. (*silence*)

HE

So, now we have a child. You and me.

(*pause*)

SHE

Yes. Yeah . . .

HE

Our child . . . I can't understand it.

SHE

Me neither.

HE

It was so strange when he came out, just when he came out of your
wonderful body . . . because he looked me straight in the eye. . . . I don't
know if it's true or if I'm imagining, but I thought that he looked at me
calmly and clearly in some way, as if he knew everything, all fucking
lies, all fucking deceits . . . everything you have to go through in life to
become a man. As if he knew everything that's going to happen to him
. . . as if he understood everything that's waiting for him . . . and as if he
knew me, as if we had always known each other, but hadn't met until
now . . . and as if he was saying, "So, there you are."

SHE

Is that why he screamed?

HE

Why do you say things like that?

SHE

I was just kidding. I'm not allowed to make a joke? Did that piss you off?

HE

It didn't sound like a joke.

SHE

What the fuck am I supposed to do?

MAN

Is that him?

GUARD

Yes, he's the one who came in this morning, just before six. Would you
like me to turn on some music?

MAN

What kind of music?

GUARD

Well, Bach or Beethoven, maybe some of his later pieces.

MAN

No, no music.

GUARD

He's the only one here. . . . He's alone.

HE

He looked at me as if he already knew everything that's going to happen
. . . everything that's waiting for him. . . . He held his hands in front of
him . . . like this . . . cupped. As if he was holding my life in his hands.

MAN

I guess he isn't . . . Is he wearing shoes?

WOMAN

Isn't he wearing his clothes?

GUARD

No, not right now. He was naked when they found him. (*silence*) Well,
should I, or would you . . .

MAN

No. . . . Yes.

SHE

I'm so tired.

(*Guard removes the sheet.*)

WOMAN

No. ("*Man*" *closes his eyes.*) No.

MAN

Isn't it him?

WOMAN

No.

MAN

Who is it? (*takes a step forward*) No. (*silence*) Poor Elias . . . Little Elias. My little Elias.

HE

Emma. (*silence*)

GUARD

Well.

MAN

Little Elias. What have you done? (*silence*)

GUARD

Is this Elias?

MAN

Yes . . . it's him. (*silence*)

GUARD

So, this is the right person?

MAN

Yes.

GUARD

You're absolutely sure?

MAN

I'm sure.

GUARD

Yes.

MAN

Of course we're sure. What the hell are you talking about? (*silence*) What the hell do you mean?

GUARD

Well, it's just that . . .

(*silence*)

MAN

I'm sorry. (*short pause*) I'm sorry.

HE

Do you want me to get him?

SHE

No . . . let him be.

GUARD

It's just that we have to be sure, so that there aren't any mistakes. Sometimes the loved ones don't see what they see. (*short pause*) It would be . . .

MAN

Yes, I see. I'm sorry.

(*Guard pulls the sheet over the dead body's face.*)

MAN

(*pulls it back again*) No. (*silence*)

GUARD

Yes, you would probably like to be by yourselves for a little while.

MAN

Yes . . . thank you.

GUARD

I'm going to . . . I'll be in the office. (*"Man" nods.*) I just had a thought.

HE

Darling.

MAN

Yes, sure. (*silence*)

GUARD

It's just a thought that I sometimes have when I take care of the deceased . . . if it is, as it sometimes is, very difficult stuff that has brought them here. . . . But I don't know if that's the case this time. I guess I'm thinking that for the deceased everything is over, they don't have to remember what has happened. For them it's over. But for us, who continue to live on, we'll remember and suffer. But for them it's over. Now they're free.

MAN

Yes.

GUARD

Yes, for them it's over. . . . Now they can rest. Maybe that's a consolation.

WOMAN

Is he supposed to lie here all alone?

HE

Hell, now we are three.

SHE

Yes.

HE

Are you happy about that?

SHE

Yes . . . but I'm not in the mood to be happy right now. Not right now.

HE

No.

SHE

You'll have to be happy for me, too.

HE

Yes, I'll try. (*silence*) (*"Woman" takes "Man's" hand and holds it.*) Yes. (*pause*) I thought that today I'll make some calls to movers and find out the costs.

SHE

But today is Saturday.

HE

Yeah, fuck, today is Saturday. Of course, the best would be if we could do the move down there ourselves. . . . It would be a lot cheaper.

SHE

We don't have that much.

HE

Yes . . . it won't be for a couple months, three months.

(*"Woman" reaches out to touch the face of the dead son. "Man" says something inaudible.*)

SHE

It's nice here. I'd like to stay here.

HE

You do?

SHE

Yes. (*silence*) I want to go to sleep . . . but it hurts so much.

HE

Are you tired, darling?

SHE

Yes . . . I've never ever felt this tired. I didn't know I could get this tired.

HE

Do you need anything? (*She shakes her head.*) It'll be incredibly nice when you come home.

SHE

I've got to go to work very soon.

HE

We don't have to talk about that now.

SHE

I want to go back to work. It's very important to me.

HE

I know. I know that it is. It's just as important for me as it is for you.

SHE

Maybe then I'll be myself again.

HE

I hope so. (*silence*)

SHE

I can't just sit somewhere out in the country and not do anything.

HE

Who said you would?

SHE

Then I'll go under.

HE

You can do whatever you want.

SHE

I won't make it.

HE

Me neither. (*silence*)

WOMAN

Is he supposed to lie here all by himself?

MAN

Emma. Let's go. (*silence*) Do you want to leave?

WOMAN

Where to?

MAN

Come on . . . Emma.

WOMAN

I'm leaving when the time is right. When the time is right I'll leave. Then
I'll leave.

MAN

Yes.

HE

Hello.

> SHE

Everything goes so fast.

> HE

What?

> SHE

Everything. Everything has gone so fast. I can't keep up.

> HE

What the hell are you talking about? Are you talking about the house again?

> SHE

Everything. I can't keep up.

> HE

But that's what we wanted. We've been driving around looking at thousands of houses.

> SHE

Because that's what you wanted. Because it was so fucking important to you.

> HE

Just for me? Did we do it just for me?

> SHE

To own a house . . . to have a child, and a family, since you never had one.

> HE

Really? (*short pause*) I thought that you wanted it too.

> SHE

I don't know what I want. I don't know anything. I don't know who I am any longer. I thought it would feel better later, once it was over, but now it just feels unreal.

> HE

What?

SHE

You, me, everything. . . . I don't know . . . as if I'd lost everything. As if I'd lost my footing. I'm longing for my nice, little apartment with its little balcony and the birch trees outside. That was my first apartment of my very own. I'm longing to go home to my grandma and my grandpa. I'm longing to sit in Grandma's lap. Longing for Grandma to pick me up and carry me to bed and tuck me in and give me a big cup of hot chocolate and a sandwich.

HE

Yes.

WOMAN

What should we do?

MAN

I don't know.

WOMAN

No . . .

HE

Well, I've had enough of the city. I've got to . . . I can't live here any longer. I want a different kind of life.

MAN

It's as if I was hearing . . .

WOMAN

I don't know how I could walk away from here and leave him with all these strangers.

MAN

No.

WOMAN

But he's always been alone. (*silence*)

MAN

I'll stay here. I won't leave. I'm staying.

SHE

We'd only known each other for a few months before I got pregnant, and now we're moving to the country. I don't know . . . it feels like everything I'm really fond of has been taken away. The only thing I've left is my work, to be able to go to work. I don't know what it'll feel like living down there with a small child. . . . I don't know a single person down there.

HE

You know me.

SHE

Well . . . do I?

HE

Yes, I hope so.

SHE

Do I know you?

HE

Yes, I hope so.

SHE

I don't know if I know you. I know certain parts of you. But I don't know if I know you.

HE

Really. (*short pause*) But . . . that's because of who you are.

SHE

You have so many dark spaces within, that I don't . . . where I don't know what you have going on.

HE

Dark spaces?

SHE

Yes.

HE

I do?

                    MAN

I hardly knew him. (*silence*)

                    HE

I have dark spaces?

                    SHE

Yes.

                    HE

What kind of fucking spaces are you talking about?

                    SHE

(*quietly*) I don't know.

                    HE

And you, yours are nice and bright?

                    SHE

They used to be.

                    WOMAN

What are we going to do? (*"Man" shakes his head.*) No . . .

                    MAN

I wish I'd known him better.

                    WOMAN

I don't know what to do. What are you supposed to do? I've never had anything like this happen to me before. (*silence*) I think we'll have to . . .

(*They look at each other.*)

                    MAN

We haven't seen each other for many years.

                    WOMAN

No.

                    MAN

You and me. I don't even know how long it's been.

WOMAN

(*quietly*) It was very long ago.

MAN

And now we see each other here. . . . Here.

HE

Yes, that's who I am.

WOMAN

Yes, I know.

MAN

What's there to say?

WOMAN

I don't know.

HE

I guess I'll go home.

SHE

Yes, I guess.

HE

Visiting hour is almost over. (*silence*) Maybe I'll stay a little longer.

MAN

Yes, we'll see . . .

WOMAN

We'll talk later about . . . what we have to talk about.

MAN

That's right. Yes.

WOMAN

I can't do it now.

MAN

Me neither.

HE

If you'd like I can stay a little longer.

SHE

No . . . there's nothing more to talk about. Nothing important.

MAN

Later we have to do something with his stuff.

WOMAN

His stuff . . .

MAN

Yes, his belongings . . . what he owned.

WOMAN

He didn't have very much.

HE

What the hell, everyone has dark spaces. Small, dark spaces. (*silence*)
You've got them too.

MAN

What did you say?

WOMAN

I can do that . . . I can take care of that. . . . It's not that much.

MAN

No . . .

HE

Emma . . .

MAN

Maybe we can do it together.

WOMAN

I can't think about that right now.

MAN

No . . .

HE

Emma . . .

MAN

But if you want me to do something with you . . .

HE

Emma . . .

WOMAN

You were hardly ever there.

SHE

Yes, what do you want?

MAN

No.

HE

Nothing.

WOMAN

I can take care of it.

MAN

Yes, but I want to . . . I bought him a new refrigerator in January. (*silence*)

HE

I never get an answer. (*silence*) From you. I never get an answer from you. You never answer me.

SHE

What kind of answer?

HE

When I say something. I don't feel that you're answering me. It's as if what I say doesn't sink in. The words don't sink in. The words don't reach you . . . don't sink into you.

SHE

What do you want me to say?

HE

When I look at you I don't feel that you're aware of that . . . that I'm looking at you. You don't see me.

SHE

Wait.

HE

Yes, what?

("Woman" turns around as if she was leaving the room. "Man" is waiting.)

MAN

There . . . (He puts his hand on her shoulder and then points to the lighted window in the door.) There's the door. . . . That's where we came in.

WOMAN

Yes.

MAN

Emma.

WOMAN

Where are we going? (silence) You should get a dog.

MAN

A dog?

WOMAN

You really should buy a dog.

MAN

Why?

WOMAN

A dog to take care of.

MAN

No, I don't want a dog.

WOMAN

A small one, a Jack Russell Terrier. That's a good kind of dog.

MAN

No, I don't want a dog.

HE

I don't know what to say.

SHE

No . . . me neither.

(*"Man" sits down.*)

MAN

I used to see him, take him to dinner, several times. I don't remember when it was, but once he said he'd figured out that he wanted to become a teacher. He said that he was applying to teachers college in the spring. I didn't notice anything. I thought everything seemed good.

WOMAN

Well then, it probably was.

MAN

What?

WOMAN

I guess he did whatever he could.

MAN

I don't understand why he didn't say anything when I saw him. Why didn't he say anything?

WOMAN

I don't know.

HE

(*stands up*) I'm leaving now.

SHE

Yes, I can see that.

HE

I'm going home.

SHE

Sure.

HE

I'll be back tonight. (*silence*) Would you like it better if I didn't come?

SHE

I'm just so fucking tired.

HE

Well, we'll talk more later.

SHE

We have to talk.

HE

Okay . . . I'll be back tonight. See you later.

SHE

We have to talk. We have to talk. (*silence*)

MAN

Are you going home?

WOMAN

I don't know. (*silence*)

MAN

What are you doing now?

WOMAN

I don't know. (*pause*) What am I supposed to do?

MAN

Yes . . .

WOMAN

I'll stay here for a while. I'll sit here for a while.

MAN

Yes. (*pause*) Do you have anyone to talk to?

WOMAN

No, not any more. . . . Do you?

MAN

No. Not anyone I can talk to. (*silence*) Do you want me to wait . . .

WOMAN

You don't have to.

MAN

I can wait for a while.

WOMAN

Why don't you leave? (*silence*)

MAN

I'll stay. I'll stay. (*silence*)

(*Everything goes dark.*)

THE END

Major Plays by Lars Norén

1979	ORESTES
1981	A TERRIBLE HAPPINESS
1981	MUNICH – ATHENS
1981	SMILES OF THE INFERNO
1982	NIGHT IS MOTHER TO THE DAY
1982	CHAOS IS THE NEIGHBOR OF GOD
1982	DEMONS
1983	THE LAST SUPPER
1984	CLAUDIO (MANTEGNA PORTOFOLIO)
1985	THE COMEDIANS
1986	FLOWERS OF OUR TIME
1987	HEBRIANA
1988	AUTUMN AND WINTER
1988	BOBBY FISCHER LIVES IN PASADENA
1988	AND GIVE US THE SHADOWS
1989	TRUTH OR DARE
1989	SUMMER
1990	LOVE MADE SIMPLE
1990	CHINNON
1991	THE LAST QUARTET
1991	LOST AND FOUND
1991	THE LEAVES IN VALLOMBROSA
1992	MOIRE DI –
1992	STERBLICH
1994	ROMANIANS
1994	BLOOD
1994	A KIND OF HADES
1994	THE CLINIC
1994	TRIO TO THE END OF THE WORLD
1997	PERSONKRETS 3:1
1998	SEVEN/THREE
1998	SHADOW BOYS
2000	NOVEMBER
2000	ACT
2000	COMING AND GOING
2002	QUIET WATERS

2003   DETAILS
2003   CHILL
2005   WAR
2006   TERMINAL
2007   ANNA POLITKOVSKIA
2010   ORESTIEN
2012   FRAGMENTE
2013   3.31.93

Acknowledgments

Once again, my deeply felt "thank you" to Jane and Richard Altschuler for their extraordinary help and support. Without their enthusiasm and dedication, this book would not have seen the light of day.

Warm "thanks" to Stan Schwartz for his keen knowledge of Swedish theater, and especially for his interest in the plays by Lars Norén. Stan is one of the few American theater people who has made the long trip to Sweden to personally experience Norén productions.

I am truly grateful for the many times my dear friend Bo Corre helped make it possible for me to try out a number of Norén translations at the Actors Studio in New York City. Also, her understanding of Norén's writing and her acting skills are without equal.

As always, I extend "a thousand thanks" to a great number of dedicated New York actors who have, over the years, shared their talents with readings and workshops, in my search for "the music" in the translations of Lars Norén's work.